one dish: two ways

one dish, two ways

Feeding the family. Without the fuss.

JANE KENNEDY

hardie grant books

Published in 2014 by Hardie Grant Books

Hardie Grant Books (Australia)
Ground Floor, Building 1
658 Church Street
Richmond, Victoria 3121
www.hardiegrant.com.au

Hardie Grant Books (UK)
Dudley House, North Suite
34–35 Southampton Street
London WC2E 7HF
www.hardiegrant.co.uk

A Cataloguing-in-Publication entry is available from the
catalogue of the National Library of Australia at www.nla.gov.au

One Dish, Two Ways: Feeding the family without the fuss
ISBN 978 1 74270 717 4

Publishing Director: Paul McNally
Project Editor: Helen Withycombe
Editor: Meelee Soorkia
Design Manager: Heather Menzies
Designer: Trisha Garner
Photographer: Mark Roper
Stylist: Deb Kaloper
Home Economist: Caroline Jones (Griffiths)
Production Manager: Todd Rechner

Colour reproduction by Splitting Image Colour Studio
Printed in China by 1010 Printing International Limited

Find this book on **Cooked.**
www.cooked.com.au
www.cooked.co.uk

Contents

It's time to add taste
and take away the stress
at family meals.

Intro

I knew one thing —
I didn't want to eat boring
plain kids' food.

Feeding a family. Every night. Is hard.

I know because I cook for seven people. Every single night.

It's not so much the physical act of cooking, although that can get pretty draining. It's coming up with the ideas for meals that everyone will eat.

It's easy cooking for adults. We love spices and chilli and herbs and zest and can dress up a boring piece of chicken or fish or steak in a flash.

But kids don't like spices and chilli and herbs and zest. *Maybe* your amazing worldly kids might, but most kids don't. Not all mine do. Green bits. Orange bits. Hot bits. Weird bits. All received with a resounding thumbs-down. And even though you may think they're being ridiculous or dramatic when they say ground black pepper is 'hot', it's 'hot' to them. So there's no point wrecking an otherwise delicious meal kids would have eaten by a careless twist of your pepper grinder.

So how do you feed everyone and keep the meal-peace?

I used to cook two shifts of food for our large family. Having five little kids at the dinner table was no Instagram moment. Dinner was NOT relaxing. There were tears, bickering, spilt drinks...often from the children as well. The banality of a 5.30 pm mealtime-slot finally led me to cook one dish for them, and one dish for us to eat later. I soon however accepted the fact my entire family should probably eat at the same time, preferably in the same postcode, possibly at the same table. I needed to shake that frying pan only ONCE a night to keep my sanity. Big Love.

There was, however, one thing I knew for sure.

There was NO WAY I was going to start eating 'plain' food just to keep the kids happy.

So I gave myself a challenge. What if I used the same base as a meal for everyone and simply jazzed it up or down? Serve the base of the meal to the kids, unadulterated if you like, but add spices and flavours and herbs to the adult version. One dish, two ways?

So here's the result.

These meals are fast and easy and not too tricky. You might have to use two bowls instead of one and two baking dishes instead of one, which just means there might be less room in the dishwasher. Boo hoo.

I love to eat the non-boombah low-carb way but that doesn't mean the kids have to. They love rice and pasta and wraps and tacos so I continue to serve it for them. Just be sensible about the amount and frequency. And if YOU don't want to eat pasta or rice or wraps or tacos, you don't have to. I've made alternative suggestions throughout the book. (Hello Cauliflower 'rice'!)

You also don't need to pile your kids' plates up to match yours. In fact *you* don't have to pile *your* plate up with food. Children do NOT eat the same amount as adults. I don't care if you say your six-year-old has the appetite of a man. He doesn't have the stomach size of a man. Give kids a smaller plate than you. And this goes for everyone – enough of the second helpings please! This book does not encourage One Dish, Two Ways, Many Times.

I've only included dinners here. I don't know many families, actually I don't know ANY families who serve an entrée before a main course every night. And I'm sure you know how to make a dessert the family loves so I haven't put a dessert section in here either. My children didn't actually know what dessert was until they started going to other people's houses. Bummer. If they're lucky they may get a bowl of vanilla ice cream, which by the way, they think is AWESOME!!

Some Rules

Vegetables don't always need to be cooked

Every night we have raw veggies on the table. Carrots, cucumber, capsicum, celery, snow peas. Crunchy raw veggies cut into sticks. SO much better than mushy overcooked unseasoned tasteless vegetables. And if your kids still won't eat a veggie at dinnertime, chop up a green apple or some watermelon or a nashi pear and serve that.

Minced meat is not just for kids

All it takes is a last-minute addition of a bit of spice and some fresh herbs and your plain meatball, hamburger patty or taco is adult-worthy. Beef, chicken, pork and veal. It's also cheap.

This is not a restaurant

It doesn't matter if some of these dishes look a bit nuts; the half-and-half look does appear kind of kooky. But remember...you're not a contestant on *MasterChef*. You do not need to 'plate up'. Relax. There are no cameras in your kitchen.

You don't have to eat the pasta

Or the rice. You're the grown-up, eat what you like but if you want to ditch the carbs at dinner time, there are plenty of alternatives I've suggested.

Kids can leave the table before you do

That extra ten or fifteen minutes while you finish a glass (or bottle) of wine at an empty table can be a game-changer. Make sure your kids take their own plates to the sink or kitchen bench.

If you're in a good mood...

Ask your children to help you prepare dinner.

It's really this simple; kids who see their parents cook will most likely be able to cook when they become grown-ups. Grown-ups who cook for themselves are less likely to become obese. Kids who see their parents swerve through a drive-through every night to pick up the family meal DO become obese.

If you're feeling a bit cranky...

Definitely, KEEP THE KIDS OUT OF THE KITCHEN until dinner is ready. And pour yourself a wine.

Kitchen Notes

When I refer to olive oil, I mean extra-virgin olive oil.

Salt is always flaky sea salt (Maldon or Murray River pink salt).

Mayonnaise is always good quality egg-based mayonnaise, like Best's.

Greek-style yoghurt is always the thick, natural yoghurt found in supermarkets.

Oven temperatures

All oven cooking temperatures in this book are for fan-forced ovens. For conventional ovens, increase the temperature by 20˚C (70°F).

Cauliflower 'Rice'

INGREDIENTS
½ cauliflower, pulled into small florets

METHOD
Put the cauliflower into a microwave-safe container with a lid. Do not add water. Microwave on full power for 5 minutes.

When the cauliflower is ready, put it in a food processor and pulse it in bursts until it starts to resemble rice.

Speedy Beetroot Relish

INGREDIENTS

1 tablespoon olive oil

1 tablespoon black mustard seeds

1 garlic clove, crushed

1 cm (⅓ inch) piece small nob of ginger, grated

1 beetroot (beet), peeled and grated (use disposable gloves to save stained fingers)

salt, to taste

1 teaspoon brown sugar

squeeze of lemon juice

1 tablespoon Greek-style yoghurt

METHOD

Heat the olive oil in a frying pan over a medium heat and add the mustard seeds. Careful, they will start to pop! Quickly add the garlic and ginger then stir in the grated beetroot and stir a little more. Add the salt, brown sugar and lemon juice and stir to mix through.

Let the mixture simmer for about 10 minutes, adding a little water to keep it moist, if necessary.

Remove from the heat and let it cool.

Add the yoghurt, mix and refrigerate until ready to serve.

Wasabi Mayonnaise

INGREDIENTS
1 tablespoon mayonnaise
1 tablespoon Greek-style yoghurt
2 cm 'worm' wasabi paste, or to taste

METHOD
Mix together all the ingredients in a small bowl and refrigerate until ready to serve.

Horseradish Hot 'Creamy' Sauce

INGREDIENTS
1 tablespoon Greek-style yoghurt
1 tablespoon prepared horseradish*
½ teaspoon hot English mustard

METHOD
Mix together all the ingredients in a small bowl and refrigerate until ready to serve.

* Use finely grated fresh horseradish instead when it's in season.

Sunday Soups & Salads

Sunday night is usually
Soup & Salad Night as my routine
is a little bit slapdash – I'm busy doing
school lunches for the next day, getting
school clothes ready, watching the telly...

These meal ideas are no fuss and easy
and have always gone down so well,
they're requested on the other
days of the week too...

Pho

Who doesn't love pho? Slices of cooked chicken and rice noodles in a yummy chicken broth. Kids can slurp this up to their hearts' content. Adults can slurp as well, after adding a flavour punch with fresh herbs, chillies, bean sprouts and a squeeze of fresh lemon. (P.S. If you are rushed for time, just get a barbecue chicken.)

INGREDIENTS

1 large organic, free-range chicken
1 litre (34 fl oz/4 cups) chicken stock
2 tablespoons fish sauce
3 cm (1¼ inch) piece ginger, grated
2 star anise
2 cinnamon sticks
1 tablespoon brown sugar
1 teaspoon freshly ground black pepper
200 g (7 oz) packet dry rice noodles
200 g (7 oz) bean sprouts

INGREDIENTS FOR ADULTS

2 spring onions (scallions), thinly sliced
½ bunch coriander (cilantro), leaves picked and chopped
crispy fried shallots, to garnish
thinly sliced red chillies, to serve
Vietnamese mint, to serve
lemon wedges, to serve

METHOD

Bring the chicken, stock, fish sauce, ginger, star anise, cinnamon, sugar, pepper and 1 litre of water to the boil in a large saucepan. Reduce the heat, cover and simmer for 1½ hours, turning the chicken over after 45 minutes.

Transfer the chicken to a chopping board. Take off the skin and discard. Use a fork to shred the chicken meat. Strain the stock then return it to the saucepan over a low–medium heat. Add the shredded chicken and simmer until the chicken is warmed through, about 3–4 minutes.

Meanwhile, prepare the noodles according to the packet instructions. Put a ladleful of noodles and a small handful of bean sprouts into each serving bowl.

1. **BOWL ONE** Scoop some broth and bits of chook into the kids' bowls and serve.

2. **BOWL TWO** Stir the spring onions and half the coriander through the remaining broth.

Add some chook pieces and herby broth to the adults' serving bowls. Serve with the shallots, chilli, mint, lemon and remaining coriander arranged on a platter for the adults (and kids) to help themselves.

SERVES 4

1.

SCOOP SOME BROTH AND BITS
OF CHOOK INTO THE KIDS' BOWLS
AND SERVE.

2.

STIR SPRING ONIONS AND CORIANDER
THROUGH THE REMAINING BROTH.
ADD SOME CHOOK PIECES AND HERBY
BROTH TO THE ADULTS' SERVING
BOWLS. SERVE WITH SHALLOTS,
CHILLI, MINT AND LEMON.

Won Ton Soup

Clear beef or chicken broth with slippery tasty mini dim sum, dressed up with baby bok choy and fresh chilli for the adults. This recipe shows you how to make your own won tons, but you could easily buy them from the freezer department of an Asian grocer (like I usually do).

INGREDIENTS

300 g (10½ oz) minced (ground) pork
2 teaspoons soy sauce
2 teaspoons oyster sauce
¼ teaspoon sesame oil
½ teaspoon rice vinegar
¼ teaspoon brown sugar
1 garlic clove, crushed
pinch of white pepper
18–24 won ton wrappers
1 litre (34 fl oz/4 cups) chicken stock

INGREDIENTS FOR ADULTS

1 spring onion (scallion), thinly sliced
1 bunch baby bok choy (pak choy), leaves separated
splash of sesame oil
1–2 red chillies, finely chopped

METHOD

Combine the pork, soy sauce, oyster sauce, sesame oil, rice vinegar, sugar, garlic and white pepper in a bowl. Place one won ton wrapper on a clean work surface or chopping board. Cover the remaining wrappers with a damp tea (dish) towel to prevent them from drying out.

Brush the edges of the won ton wrapper with a little water. Place a heaped teaspoon of the pork mixture in the centre. Lift up the edges and twist to seal – it should look like a money bag. Repeat with the remaining wrappers and filling.

Bring a large saucepan of water to the boil over a high heat. Add the won tons and cook for 5–7 minutes, or until the won tons rise to the top and the filling is cooked through.

While the won tons are cooking, bring the chicken stock to the boil in a saucepan over a high heat then reduce to a gentle simmer.

When the won tons are ready, remove them using a slotted spoon and drain on a tea (dish) towel.

1. **BOWL ONE** Put half of the won tons into the stock and heat for 1 minute. To serve, divide the won tons among the kids' bowls and ladle over some stock.

2. **BOWL TWO** For the grown-ups, increase the heat to medium and add the spring onion and bok choy. Cook until the bok choy turns a vibrant green, about 2 minutes. Add the remaining won tons and heat through.

Remove the saucepan from the heat and stir in the sesame oil. To serve, ladle the soup and won tons into bowls and scatter over the chilli.

SERVES 4

PUT HALF OF THE WON TONS INTO THE
STOCK AND HEAT FOR 1 MINUTE. TO SERVE,
DIVIDE THE WON TONS AMONG THE KIDS'
BOWLS AND LADLE OVER SOME STOCK.

2.

FOR THE GROWN-UPS, ADD SPRING ONION AND BOK CHOY. COOK UNTIL THE BOK CHOY TURNS A VIBRANT GREEN. ADD THE WON TONS, STIR IN SESAME OIL AND SERVE.

French Onion Soup

Leave the onions for the adults to enjoy and serve the broth to the kids. Top both bowls with toasted cheesy bread.

INGREDIENTS
80 g (2¾ oz) butter, coarsely chopped
1 tablespoon olive oil
2 kg (4 lb 6 oz) onions, thinly sliced
1 litre (34 fl oz/4 cups) beef stock
5 thyme sprigs
3 parsley sprigs
2 fresh bay leaves
salt and freshly ground black pepper
8 × 1 cm (½ inch) thick slices of baguette
130 g (4½ oz/1 cup) grated gruyere

METHOD
Melt the butter with the oil in a large heavy-based saucepan over a medium heat. Add the onions, cover and cook for 20 minutes, stirring occasionally.

Remove the lid, lower the heat and cook, stirring occasionally, for about 45 minutes, or until the onions begin to caramelise.

Add the stock, a little at a time.

Tie the herbs together with kitchen string and add them to the saucepan. Season the soup with salt and pepper. Bring it to the boil then reduce the heat and simmer gently for another 40 minutes, scraping the base occasionally to remove any caramelised onion.

To make the cheesy toasts, preheat the oven to 200°C (400°F/Gas 6). Sprinkle the cheese on the slices of bread and bake for 5 minutes, or until the cheese is bubbling.

Meanwhile, strain the soup and reserve the onion.

1.
BOWL ONE Ladle the strained broth into the kids' bowls. Top with a piece of cheesy toast and serve straight away.

2.
BOWL TWO Put a little of the reserved onion into the adults' bowls and ladle in the broth. Top with the cheesy toasts and serve.

SERVES 4

Orange Soup

Bright and tasty orange soup is given a spicy kick for the grown-ups just before serving.

INGREDIENTS
60 ml (2 fl oz/¼ cup) vegetable oil
4 carrots, peeled and thinly sliced
1 onion, finely chopped
6 garlic cloves, crushed
2 cm (¾ inch) piece ginger, grated
1 litre low-salt (34 fl oz/4 cups) chicken stock
60 ml (2 fl oz/¼ cup) light coconut milk
juice of 1 large orange, zest of ½
salt

INGREDIENTS FOR ADULTS
1 teaspoon ground cumin
freshly ground black pepper, to taste
60 g (2 oz/¼ cup) Greek-style yoghurt or
  sour cream
chopped coriander (cilantro), to serve

METHOD
Heat the vegetable oil in a large saucepan over a medium heat. Add the carrots, onion, garlic and ginger and cook, stirring occasionally, for about 6–8 minutes, or until the onion is golden.

Add the stock, coconut milk, half of the orange juice and the orange zest and bring to the boil. Reduce the heat to low–medium, cover and cook, stirring occasionally, for about 20 minutes, or until the carrots are tender.

Using a food processor or blender, purée the soup in batches until smooth then return it to the saucepan over a medium heat. Stir in the remaining orange juice and add salt to taste. Cook for a further 2–3 minutes, or until heated through.

1. **BOWL ONE** Serve out the kids' version into bowls.

2. **BOWL TWO** To the remaining soup, add the cumin and lots of freshly ground black pepper. Serve garnished with a dollop of yoghurt or sour cream and some coriander.

SERVES 4

Italian 'Lasagne' Soup

Lasagne is a favourite in our house but sometimes it's just a bit too heavy. I do love the flavour combo though and so do the kids. They also love soup. This soupy lighter version works really well...and can be served with or without the pasta for grown-ups.

INGREDIENTS

1 tablespoon olive oil
3 garlic cloves, crushed
1 onion, chopped
6 Italian pork sausages (not spicy)
1 teaspoon dried oregano
800 g (1 lb 2 oz) tin chopped tomatoes
1 litre (34 fl oz/4 cups) chicken stock
200 g (7 oz) dry pappardelle or
  'broken' bits of lasagne sheets
salt
grated low-fat mozzarella, to serve

INGREDIENTS FOR ADULTS

60 g (2 oz/¼ cup) ricotta
zest of ½ lemon
freshly ground black pepper
chopped flat-leaf (Italian) parsley, to serve

METHOD

Heat the olive oil in a large saucepan over a medium heat. Sauté the garlic and onion until translucent. Squeeze the sausage meat out of the skins and crumble the meat into the saucepan. Don't break it up too much – stir it around gently until it's just brown, about 3–4 minutes. Add the oregano and tomatoes and simmer for 5 minutes.

Pour in the stock and bring to the boil. Reduce the heat and simmer for about 30 minutes. Add the pasta and cook for another 10 minutes, or until the pasta is al dente. Season with salt.

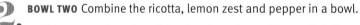

1. **BOWL ONE** Ladle the soup into the kids' bowls, top with a little mozzarella and serve.

2. **BOWL TWO** Combine the ricotta, lemon zest and pepper in a bowl.

Ladle the soup into the adults' bowls and top with small dollops of the ricotta mixture. Sprinkle with some parsley and serve.

SERVES 4

1.

LADLE THE SOUP INTO THE KIDS'
BOWLS, TOP WITH A LITTLE
MOZARELLA AND SERVE.

2.

COMBINE THE RICOTTA, LEMON
ZEST AND PEPPER IN A BOWL. LADLE
THE SOUP INTO THE ADULTS'
BOWLS AND TOP WITH DOLLOPS
OF THE RICOTTA MIXTURE.

Green Soup

I just call this Green Soup. No one seems to ever ask why it's green!
The simple addition of chopped chives and a dollop of yoghurt is enough
to jazz this up for the adults.

INGREDIENTS
60 g (2 oz/¼ cup) unsalted butter
1 onion, chopped
1 litre (34 fl oz/4 cups) low-salt vegetable
   stock
850 g (1 lb 14 oz) shelled fresh peas or
   frozen peas, thawed
3 tablespoons chopped flat-leaf (Italian)
   parsley
3 tablespoons chopped mint
salt

INGREDIENTS FOR ADULTS
½ teaspoon ground cumin
½ teaspoon hot paprika
60 g (2 oz/¼ cup) Greek-style yoghurt
freshly snipped chives, to garnish
freshly ground black pepper

METHOD
Melt the butter in a heavy-based saucepan over a medium heat. Cook the onion
until translucent, for around 6–8 minutes. Add half the stock and bring to the
boil. Add the peas, lower the heat, and simmer until the peas are tender – about
5 minutes for fresh peas or 2–3 minutes for frozen peas.

Remove the saucepan from the heat and stir through the parsley, mint and
remaining stock and add salt to taste.

Purée the soup in a blender and if it's too thick thin it with a little water.

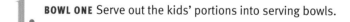

1. **BOWL ONE** Serve out the kids' portions into serving bowls.

2. **BOWL TWO** For the adults, return the remaining soup to the saucepan. Add the cumin
and paprika and simmer over a medium heat for 2–3 minutes.

To serve, add a dollop of yoghurt, some chives and lots of pepper.

SERVES 4

1.
SERVE OUT THE KIDS' GREEN
SOUP INTO SERVING BOWLS.

2.

ADD CUMIN AND PAPRIKA TO THE
ADULTS' SOUP. TO SERVE, ADD A
DOLLOP OF YOGHURT, SOME CHIVES
AND LOTS OF PEPPER.

Chicken Cobb Salad

An American classic – chicken, greens, avocado, tomatoes, eggs, bacon...what more could you want? I serve this on a big platter and everyone chooses their own combination.

INGREDIENTS

600 g (1 lb 5 oz) boneless, skinless chicken breasts

250 ml (8½ fl oz/1 cup) store-bought teriyaki sauce

4 large soft-boiled eggs, cut in half lengthways

1 tablespoon red wine vinegar

60 ml (2 fl oz/¼ cup) olive oil

salt and freshly ground black pepper

60 ml (2 fl oz/¼ cup) vegetable oil

6 bacon rashers

1 baby cos (romaine) lettuce, leaves separated

1 telegraph (long) cucumber, halved lengthways and cut into ½ cm (¼ inch) thick slices

2 avocados, stoned and thickly sliced

2 tomatoes, cut into wedges

250 g (9 oz) feta cheese, cubed

METHOD

Coat the chicken with the teriyaki sauce and leave it to marinate in the fridge for 1 hour.

While the chicken is marinating, prepare the red wine vinaigrette. Mix together the vinegar and olive oil. Add salt and pepper to taste and set aside.

Heat 2 tablespoons of the vegetable oil in a frying pan over a medium heat. Fry the chicken for about 7–8 minutes per side, or until cooked through.

While the chicken is cooking, heat the remaining vegetable oil in a separate frying pan and cook the bacon over a medium heat for 3–4 minutes per side, or until crispy.

When cooked, cut the chicken into thick slices on the diagonal.

Make a bed of lettuce leaves on a large platter. Arrange the chicken, eggs, bacon, cucumber, avocado, tomato and feta on top, in separate sections, so that everyone can choose their own cobb salad ingredients. Serve with the red wine vinaigrette.

SERVES 4

Caesar 'Salad' Eggy Toasts

A different way to serve eggs on toast. The dressing can be served on the side for adults, and those who love anchovies (like I do) can add extra on their lettuce wedges.

INGREDIENTS
40 g (1½ oz) butter
4 slices of wholemeal (wholewheat) bread
4 large eggs
salt and freshly ground black pepper
grated parmesan, to serve
1 iceberg lettuce, cut into wedges

Caesar dressing
60 g (2 oz/¼ cup) mayonnaise
2–3 teaspoons lemon juice

½ teaspoon dijon mustard
dash of worcestershire sauce
2 anchovy fillets in oil
½ small garlic clove, crushed
1 tablespoon grated parmesan
salt and freshly ground black pepper

INGREDIENTS FOR ADULTS
flat-leaf (Italian) parsley leaves, to serve
4 anchovy fillets in oil

METHOD
To make the caesar dressing, combine the mayonnaise, lemon juice, mustard, worcestershire sauce, anchovies, garlic and parmesan in a small bowl. Add salt and pepper to taste and set aside.

Heat a large frying pan over a low–medium heat. Butter both sides of the bread slices and cut a hole in the centre of each slice. Toast one side of the bread in the pan until lightly golden, then flip and reduce the heat to low. One by one, crack the eggs into a cup and gently slide them into the bread holes. Fry on a very low heat until the eggs look done.

Using a spatula, transfer the egg toasts to paper towels.

1. **DISH ONE** Sprinkle the egg toasts with parmesan and serve with the lettuce wedges and the dressing on the side.

2. **DISH TWO** Season the eggs with salt and pepper and top with a little parmesan. Serve with the lettuce wedges garnished with parsley and extra anchovy fillets.

SERVES 4

1.

SPRINKLE THE EGG TOASTS WITH
PARMESAN AND SERVE WITH
THE LETTUCE WEDGES AND THE
DRESSING ON THE SIDE.

2.

SEASON THE EGGS WITH SALT
AND PEPPER AND TOP WITH
A LITTLE PARMESAN. SERVE
WITH THE LETTUCE WEDGES
GARNISHED WITH PARSLEY AND
EXTRA ANCHOVY FILLETS.

Grilled BLT Salad

A bacon, lettuce and tomato sandwich is a childhood favourite of mine. And anything that mentions the word 'bacon' gets the big thumbs up. This version uses grilled cos lettuce as the 'bread' for the grown-ups and pitta for the kids.

INGREDIENTS
60 ml (2 fl oz/¼ cup) olive oil
1 tablespoon white wine vinegar
salt and freshly ground black pepper
35 g (1¼ oz/¼ cup) crumbled feta
4 bacon rashers
2 pitta breads
olive oil, for brushing
2 tomatoes, sliced
lettuce leaves, to serve

INGREDIENTS FOR ADULTS
2 baby cos (romaine) lettuces, halved lengthways
olive oil, for brushing

METHOD
Whisk together the olive oil, vinegar, salt and pepper in a bowl. Stir through the feta and set aside.

Heat a non-stick frying pan over a medium heat. Cook the bacon for 3–4 minutes per side, or until crispy.

1. **DISH ONE** Heat a chargrill pan over a medium heat. Brush the pitta breads lightly with oil and grill for 2 minutes per side, or until they are nicely toasted and have grill marks.

Top with the tomato, lettuce leaves and bacon and serve the dressing on the side as an option for the kids to try.

2. **DISH TWO** Brush the cos lettuce halves with oil and grill for 2 minutes per side, or until they are just wilted and have grill marks.

Put one lettuce half on each grown-up's plate and drizzle with a small amount of the dressing. Arrange a strip of crispy bacon and 3 tomato slices over each lettuce half. Drizzle over the remaining dressing and serve while the lettuce is warm.

SERVES 4

Greek Salad with Risoni

I love Greek salad and could eat it every night...and often do. Half of the kids love it as well...the other half love some of the ingredients.

One thing they all love is risoni. Thanks to food writer Phoodie for this great way to jazz up a very traditional dish with this fab twist. You'll know what ingredients your kids will like/not like. I make two bowls...one with cucumber, capsicum, tomato, feta and risoni and the other one as directed below – with the lot.

INGREDIENTS

330 g (11½ oz/1½ cups) risoni

juice of 2 lemons, plus extra to serve

60 ml (2 fl oz/¼ cup) olive oil, plus extra for drizzling

salt and freshly ground black pepper

2 telegraph (long) cucumbers, sliced

1 large red capsicum (pepper), cut into strips

1 small green capsicum (pepper), cut into strips

250 g (9 oz) grape tomatoes, halved

200 g (7 oz) feta

INGREDIENTS FOR ADULTS

100 g (3½ oz) unpitted kalamata olives

½ bunch spring onions (scallions), finely chopped

½ small red onion, thinly sliced

1 teaspoon dried oregano

METHOD

Bring a saucepan of salted water to the boil. Cook the risoni as per the packet instructions. It is VERY important not to overcook it as it will become gluggy and stick together – GROSS. Once cooked, refresh in cold water and toss through the lemon juice and olive oil. Add salt and pepper to taste and set aside.

Mix the cucumbers, capsicums and tomatoes in a bowl, then divide them into two serving bowls.

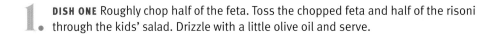

1. **DISH ONE** Roughly chop half of the feta. Toss the chopped feta and half of the risoni through the kids' salad. Drizzle with a little olive oil and serve.

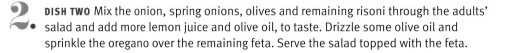

2. **DISH TWO** Mix the onion, spring onions, olives and remaining risoni through the adults' salad and add more lemon juice and olive oil, to taste. Drizzle some olive oil and sprinkle the oregano over the remaining feta. Serve the salad topped with the feta.

SERVES 4 AS A MAIN COURSE

1.

TOSS THE CHOPPED FETA AND HALF OF THE RISONI THROUGH THE KIDS' SALAD. DRIZZLE WITH A LITTLE OLIVE OIL AND SERVE.

2.

MIX THE ONION, SPRING ONIONS, OLIVES AND RISONI THROUGH THE ADULTS' SALAD AND ADD MORE LEMON JUICE AND OLIVE OIL, TO TASTE. DRIZZLE OLIVE OIL AND SPRINKLE OREGANO OVER THE REMAINING FETA AND SERVE.

Crunchy Chicken & Quinoa Salad

Thanks to Sam Ward from Perth Mexican restaurant el Público for this recipe.

I've recently introduced quinoa to the house and it's slowly getting the thumbs up! The crunch of the chia seeds works well and the onion and radish gives a lift to the grown-ups' dish.

INGREDIENTS

400 g (14 oz) boneless, skinless
    chicken breasts
150 g (5½ oz/¾ cup) white quinoa
2–3 teaspoons black chia seeds

Recado verde

1 bunch coriander (cilantro)
1 bunch flat-leaf (Italian) parsley
100 ml (3½ fl oz) canola oil
2½ tablespoons malt vinegar
2 teaspoons ground allspice

2 teaspoons ground coriander
½ teaspoon ground cumin
¼ teaspoon ground cinnamon
juice and zest of 1 orange

INGREDIENTS FOR ADULTS

juice of ½ lime
½ red onion, shaved on a mandolin
1 radish, shaved on a mandolin
1 cup coriander (cilantro) leaves,
    loosely packed

METHOD

Bring a saucepan of water to the boil. Steam the chicken, covered, in a steamer insert arranged over the saucepan, for 10 minutes. Turn the chicken and cook for 10 minutes on the other side, or until it is cooked through.

While the chicken is steaming, prepare the quinoa according to the packet instructions.

To prepare the *recado verde*, combine all the ingredients in a food processor. Add salt and pepper to taste and set aside.

Remove the chicken from the steamer and allow it to cool. Slice the chicken on the diagonal and divide into two serving bowls. Add half of the quinoa and half of the chia seeds to each bowl.

1. **BOWL ONE** Drizzle a little *recado verde* – not too much – over the kids' salad and serve.

2. **BOWL TWO** Add the lime juice, onion, radish and coriander to the grown-ups' salad and toss to combine. Drizzle with the *recado verde* and serve.

SERVES 4

1.

DRIZZLE A LITTLE RECADO VERDE
– NOT TOO MUCH – OVER THE
KIDS' SALAD AND SERVE.

2.

ADD LIME JUICE, ONION,
RADISH AND CORIANDER
TO THE GROWN-UPS'
SALAD AND TOSS. DRIZZLE
WITH THE RECADO VERDE
AND SERVE.

Hummus Salad

We all love hummus but I liked the idea of a salad using all the ingredients that go into hummus before it gets mashed up. Chickpeas are known in our house as 'hummus balls'. This is a tasty different salad with crunch. And of course I add a hint of fresh chilli for added flavour for me.

INGREDIENTS

1 large pitta bread
olive oil, for brushing
400 g (14 oz) tin chickpeas, drained and rinsed
1 red onion, chopped
½ red capsicum (pepper), chopped
½ telegraph (long) cucumber, chopped
1 celery stalk, chopped

Tahini dressing
60 ml (2 fl oz/¼ cup) lemon juice
60 ml (2 fl oz/¼ cup) olive oil
65 g (2 oz/¼ cup) tahini
1 garlic clove, crushed
salt and freshly ground black pepper

INGREDIENTS FOR ADULTS

1 teaspoon sesame seeds
1 teaspoon cumin seeds
1 teaspoon coriander seeds, crushed
½ teaspoon chilli flakes

METHOD

To make the dressing, whisk together the lemon juice, olive oil, tahini and garlic in a medium bowl. Season with salt and pepper. If needed, add a little water to make the dressing a bit runnier.

Heat a chargrill pan over a medium heat. Lightly brush the pitta with olive oil, then grill for 2 minutes per side, or until crispy. Tear into small pieces and set aside.

Divide the chickpeas between four bowls. Arrange the chopped vegetables in bowls on the table with spoons so everyone can add their preferred veggies to their salad.

1. **DISH ONE** After the kids have chosen their vegetables, pour over a little dressing and let them combine the salad. Top with some pitta pieces.

2. **DISH TWO** In a dry frying pan over a medium heat, toast the sesame, coriander and cumin seeds until fragrant. Transfer to a small bowl and mix through the chilli flakes.

Toss the dressing through the adults' salads and top with torn-up pieces of pitta and the spicy sesame seed mixture.

SERVES 4

Pasta, Noodles & More

The kids would eat spaghetti bol
every night...if they could. I don't have a real
problem with that except it's a bit...BORING.
Here's a selection of some pasta
and noodle dishes that are
just a bit different.

Pasta with Homemade Tomato Sauce & Mussels

Simple. Spaghetti napolitana for the kids, and delicious spicy mussels for you! I usually skip the pasta altogether and serve the dish with a simple green salad. Too easy.

INGREDIENTS
100 ml (3½ fl oz) olive oil
4 garlic cloves, crushed
2 onions, finely chopped
2 carrots, finely diced
1 teaspoon dried oregano
800 g (1 lb 12 oz) tin chopped tomatoes
1 teaspoon salt
200 g (7 oz) dried spaghetti
grated parmesan, to serve

INGREDIENTS FOR ADULTS
2 teaspoons capers, rinsed
1 tablespoon olive oil
1 garlic clove, crushed
2 small red chillies, chopped
125 ml (4 fl oz/½ cup) white wine
12 mussels, washed and debearded
chopped flat-leaf (Italian) parsley, to serve
salad leaves, to serve

METHOD
Heat the olive oil in a large saucepan over a medium heat. Stir-fry the garlic and onion for about 1 minute. Add the carrots and oregano and cook for 5–7 minutes, stirring occasionally, until the vegetables are slightly brown. Add the tomatoes, salt and 250 ml (8½ fl oz/1 cup) of water and bring to the boil. Lower the heat and simmer uncovered for about 45 minutes, stirring occasionally, until the sauce has thickened.

1. **DISH ONE** Bring a saucepan of salted water to the boil. Cook the pasta according to the packet instructions, then drain.

Transfer half the sauce to a bowl and stir through the pasta until it is well coated. Divide into serving bowls and top with some grated parmesan.

2. **DISH TWO** To the remaining sauce, add the capers.

Heat the olive oil in a frying pan over a medium heat. Add the garlic and half the chilli and sauté for about 30 seconds. Add the white wine, let it sizzle for about 10 seconds then add the remaining tomato sauce. Cover, increase the heat to high and bring to the boil.

Add the mussels and cook for 3 minutes with the lid on, still over a high heat. Stir once gently, and cook for a further 3 minutes, or until the mussels are cooked and have opened completely. Discard any mussels that have not opened.

Garnish with fresh parsley and the remaining fresh chilli and serve straight away.

SERVES 4

1.
PLAIN AND SIMPLE NAPOLI SAUCE
WITH PASTA AND PARMESAN
FOR THE KIDS.

2.

MUSSELS IN A RICH TOMATO SAUCE
WITH GARLIC, CHILLI, CAPERS AND
WHITE WINE FOR ADULTS.

Lasagne Carbonara

This is a different way to serve bacon and eggs...a combo that's morphed into a pasta dish. For grown-ups, I add lots of freshly cracked pepper and sea salt, parmesan and parsley.

INGREDIENTS
6 prosciutto slices or 6 very thinly sliced
   bacon rashers
40 g (1½ oz) butter
salt
1 tablespoon white vinegar
6 eggs
4 fresh lasagne sheets (10 cm/4 inches long)
grated parmesan, to serve

INGREDIENTS FOR ADULTS
splash of white wine
squeeze of lemon juice
salt and freshly ground black pepper
chilli flakes, to serve
chopped flat-leaf (Italian) parsley, to serve

METHOD
In a non-stick frying pan, cook the prosciutto or bacon over a medium heat until crispy. Remove from the pan and keep warm. Add the butter to the pan and keep warm over the lowest heat.

Bring a saucepan of salted water to the boil over a high heat. Add the vinegar and reduce the heat to low–medium to maintain a gentle simmer.

Crack the eggs into 6 small cups. Give the water a good circular stir, then tip 1 egg at a time into the centre of the swirling water. Simmer the eggs until the whites are white and the yolks remain soft, about 3 minutes. Using a slotted spoon, transfer the eggs to a clean tea towel to drain.

Bring another saucepan of salted water to the boil. Reduce to a medium–high heat and cook the sheets of pasta for 2–3 minutes, or until just tender. Remove the pasta with a slotted spatula, allowing it to drain for a few seconds.

Lay out the pasta sheets on four warmed plates and top with 1 poached egg each for the kids and 2 eggs each for the adults.

1. **DISH ONE** Top each of the kids' plates with a slice of the prosciutto or bacon and one-third of the butter. Serve with some grated parmesan.

2. **DISH TWO** Heat the frying pan with the remaining butter over a high heat and add the wine and lemon juice. Let it bubble for 1 minute, then remove from the heat. Divide the sauce and the remaining proscuitto or bacon between the adults' plates. Season with salt and pepper and serve with parmesan, chilli flakes and fresh parsley.

SERVES 4

Tortellini with Roast Pumpkin Sauce

I'm not a fan of 'hiding' vegetables to be honest, but the kids just call this 'orange tortellini'.

INGREDIENTS

350 g (12½ oz) pumpkin (winter squash), peeled and cut into large cubes
2 tablespoons olive oil
salt and freshly ground black pepper
500 g (1 lb 2 oz) store-bought cheese tortellini
20 g unsalted butter
1 small onion, finely chopped
pinch of freshly grated nutmeg
300 ml pouring cream
25 g (1 oz/¼ cup) grated parmesan, plus extra to serve

INGREDIENTS FOR ADULTS

handful of baby spinach leaves
50 g (1¾ oz) sharp blue cheese, crumbled
chopped flat-leaf (Italian) parsley, to serve

METHOD

Preheat the oven to 180°C (350°/Gas 4).

Put the pumpkin on a baking tray, drizzle with the olive oil and season with salt and pepper. Roast for about 25–30 minutes, or until soft. Remove the pumpkin from the oven and purée in a food processor or blender. Set aside.

Bring a large saucepan of salted water to the boil. Add the tortellini and cook according to the packet instructions. Reserve 125 ml (4 fl oz/½ cup) of the cooking liquid before draining the pasta.

Meanwhile, heat the butter in a frying pan over a medium–high heat. Sauté the onion until translucent, then add the pumpkin purée and nutmeg and cook for 1 minute. Stir in the cream and bring to a simmer. Reduce the heat to low–medium and stir the sauce continuously until it thickens slightly. Add the parmesan and cook for about 1 minute more. Remove from the heat.

1. **DISH ONE** In a saucepan over a medium heat, combine half the tortellini with half the sauce and cook until the pasta is warmed through. If necessary, add some of the reserved cooking water to loosen. Divide among the kids' serving bowls, top with extra parmesan and serve.

2. **DISH TWO** Heat the remaining tortellini and sauce in the saucepan until the pasta is warmed through, then stir through the baby spinach until wilted. Sprinkle with the blue cheese and parsley and serve.

SERVES 6

1.

TOSS THE TORTELLINI WITH THE
PUMPKIN SAUCE, TOP WITH FRESHLY
GRATED PARMESAN AND SERVE.

2.

STIR THE BABY SPINACH THROUGH
THE PASTA AND PUMPKIN SAUCE.
SPRINKLE WITH BLUE CHEESE AND
FRESH PARSLEY AND SERVE.

Open Ricotta Ravioli with Asparagus

Open ravioli is so much easier than doing the real thing and looks impressive! Only half of the kids are into asparagus so I delete that final touch and they just have the cheesy ravioli by itself.

INGREDIENTS

500 g (1 lb 2 oz) fresh asparagus, trimmed and cut into 3 cm (1¼ inch) pieces
100 g (3½ oz) mascarpone
100 g (3½ oz) ricotta
25 g (1 oz/¼ cup) parmesan, plus extra to serve
salt
4 dry lasagne sheets

125 g (4½ oz) unsalted butter, for garnish
100 g (3½ oz) slivered almonds

INGREDIENTS FOR ADULTS

1 anchovy fillet in oil, very finely chopped
½ garlic clove, crushed
pinch of cayenne pepper
freshly ground black pepper
grated lemon zest, to serve

METHOD

To prepare the filling, bring a saucepan of salted water to the boil over a high heat. Blanch the asparagus for 2 minutes then cool straight away in icy water. Reserve some of the tips for topping the adults' dish. Purée the remaining asparagus in a food processor then transfer to a bowl. Add the cheeses and a pinch of salt and combine.

Bring another saucepan of salted water to the boil. Add the pasta sheets and cook according to the packet instructions. While the pasta is cooking, put the asparagus and cheese filling in a large stainless steel bowl and heat it over the boiling pasta water.

Melt the butter in a frying pan over a medium heat. Add the almonds and cook, shaking frequently for about 5 minutes, or until the butter is light brown. Immediately remove the almonds and butter to a bowl to stop the browning process.

1. **DISH ONE** To serve, tear a sheet of pasta in half and put one half on a plate. Add a generous amount of the filling and top with the other half of the pasta sheet. Repeat to make another kids' serve. Drizzle over some brown butter and almonds and top with extra parmesan.

2. **DISH TWO** To the remaining cheese mixture, add the anchovy, garlic, cayenne pepper and salt and pepper to taste and combine.

To serve, tear a sheet of pasta in half and put one half on a plate. Top with a generous spoonful of the filling and cover with the other half of the pasta sheet. Repeat to make another adults' serve. Garnish the ravioli with the reserved asparagus spears and spoon over some brown butter and almonds. Add a grind of black pepper and sprinkle over the lemon zest and extra parmesan.

SERVES 4

1.

CHEESY RAVIOLI WITH BUTTER
AND ALMONDS FOR THE KIDS.

2.

ADD ANCHOVIES, GARLIC AND THE CAYENNE
PEPPER TO THE CHEESY ASPARAGUS FILLING.
SERVE THE RAVIOLI WITH ASPARAGUS SPEARS,
BROWN BUTTER, ALMONDS AND LEMON ZEST.

Mac & Cheese with Crispy Bacon Bits

This version of mac and cheese involves two ovenproof dishes – one uses pasta for the kids, the other uses cauliflower for the grown-ups.

INGREDIENTS

200 g (7 oz) macaroni, shells or penne
50 g (1¾ oz) unsalted butter,
  plus extra for topping
50 g (1¾ oz) plain (all-purpose) flour
750 ml (25½ fl oz/3 cups) milk
125 g (4½ oz/1 cup) grated cheddar
250 g bacon (9 oz), finely chopped
  and cooked until golden and crisp
60 g (2 oz/1 cup) panko crumbs

INGREDIENTS FOR ADULTS

½ cauliflower, cut into florets and
  steamed until tender
1 teaspoon cayenne pepper
1 teaspoon dijon mustard

METHOD

Preheat the oven to 180°C (350°F/Gas 4).

Cook the pasta according to the packet instructions, then drain.

Meanwhile, melt the butter in a saucepan over a medium heat. Add the flour and stir continuously for about 1 minute. Add the milk a little at a time, stirring constantly, until you have a white sauce. Add the cheese and continue to stir quickly until the cheese has melted, about 1 minute. Keep the sauce warm.

1. **DISH ONE** Put the cooked pasta in one baking dish and pour over half the cheesy sauce. Sprinkle with half of each of the bacon and breadcrumbs, and dot with little knobs of butter. Bake for 20 minutes, or until golden and bubbly.

2. **DISH TWO** Add the cauliflower to the other baking dish. Add the cayenne pepper and mustard to the remaining cheese sauce then pour it over the cauliflower. Sprinkle with the remaining bacon and breadcrumbs, and place little knobs of butter on top. Bake for 20 minutes, or until golden and bubbly.

SERVES 4

Quick Stix Bolognese

You'll need a vegetable spiraliser to make the 'veggie spaghetti' for this one. You can buy them at kitchenware stores.

INGREDIENTS
1 tablespoon olive oil
1 garlic clove, crushed
500 g (1 lb 2 oz) minced (ground) beef
350 ml (12 fl oz) tomato passata (puréed tomatoes)
salt
200 g (7 oz) spaghetti, or any type of pasta
grated parmesan, to serve

INGREDIENTS FOR ADULTS
¼ teaspoon chilli flakes
freshly ground black pepper
chopped flat-leaf (Italian) parsley, to serve

Veggie spaghetti
1 zucchini (courgette)
1 carrot

METHOD
Heat a non-stick frying pan over a medium heat. Add the olive oil and garlic and gently cook for about 1 minute, stirring constantly. Add the minced beef and cook, stirring to break it up, for about 5 minutes, or until brown.

Pour in the passata, season with salt and stir well. Cover and simmer for 15 minutes, adding a little water if needed to keep it moist.

1.

DISH ONE While the sauce is simmering, bring a saucepan of salted water to the boil and cook the pasta according to the packet instructions.

To serve, top the pasta with some bolognese sauce and scatter over some parmesan.

2.

DISH TWO While the bolognese is cooking, prepare the 'veggie spaghetti' for adults. Using a vegetable spiraliser, turn the zucchini and carrot into 'spaghetti'. Microwave on high for 2 minutes, or until just tender.

To the remaining bolognese, add the chilli flakes and pepper. Top the steamed 'veggie spaghetti' with the sauce, some grated parmesan and freshly chopped parsley.

SERVES 4

'Exploding' Pork Dumplings with Snow Peas

I call these 'exploding' dumplings as they are a deconstructed version. Adults can leave out the won ton wrappers and add chunks of flash-fried cabbage. This dish is also great with Nuoc cham dipping sauce (page 96).

INGREDIENTS

1 tablespoon vegetable oil
3 garlic cloves, crushed
4 cm (1½ inch) piece ginger, grated
500 g (1 lb 2 oz) minced (ground) pork
large handful of snow peas (mangetout),
  shredded
1 carrot, grated
2 tablespoons rice vinegar
salt
6 won ton wrappers

INGREDIENTS FOR ADULTS

¼ teaspoon sesame oil
1 tablespoon vegetable oil
100 g (3½ oz) green cabbage, chopped
2 birdseye chillies, finely chopped
2 tablespoons chopped roasted peanuts
2 spring onions (scallions), shredded

METHOD

Heat the vegetable oil in a frying pan over a medium heat. Add the garlic and ginger and cook for 1 minute.

Add the minced pork, stirring continuously to break it up. Once the meat has changed colour and is cooked through, stir in the snow peas and cook for a further 1–2 minutes.

Stir in the carrot and vinegar and season with salt. Turn off the heat and set aside half of the pork mixture.

1. **DISH ONE** Bring a saucepan of water to the boil. Cook the won ton wrappers one at a time for about 1 minute each, then transfer to the pan with the cooked pork mixture. Once all the won ton wrappers are cooked, toss everything in the pan and serve out the kids' meals.

2. **DISH TWO** Heat the sesame and vegetable oils in a frying pan over a high heat. Flash-fry the cabbage until just tender, then add the chilli and peanuts. Toss for 1 minute, then return the reserved pork to the pan. Heat through for about 2 minutes, stirring constantly.

Divide into serving bowls and garnish with the spring onions.

SERVES 4

Pasta Reale

This recipe is inspired by Italian chef Michela Chiappa's pasta reale, a traditional peasant-style pasta soup dish which is incredibly easy to prepare. I have to say the kids love watching the part where I grate in the 'pasta tails'.

This is a serving for ONE!

INGREDIENTS
250 ml (8½ fl oz/1 cup) chicken stock
1 egg
salt and freshly ground black pepper
50 g (1¾ oz/½ cup) grated parmesan, plus
   extra to serve
50 g (1¾ oz/½ cup) dry breadcrumbs

INGREDIENTS FOR ADULTS
¼ teaspoon dried chilli flakes (optional)
¼ teaspoon cayenne pepper
handful of baby spinach leaves

METHOD
Bring the chicken stock to the boil in a saucepan over a medium–high heat.

Crack the egg into a bowl and whisk with a little salt and pepper. Add the parmesan and breadcrumbs and mix to form a dough. Refrigerate for 30 minutes to let it firm up.

Using the large holes of a cheese grater, grate the dough over the chicken broth so that the pasta tails drop straight in. (If you're getting steam burns, lower the heat!) Return to a simmer for about 1–2 minutes.

1. **DISH ONE** Serve with lots of freshly grated parmesan.

2. **DISH TWO** For adults, stir in the chilli flakes, if using, cayenne pepper and spinach leaves through the soup until the spinach wilts. Top with freshly grated parmesan.

SERVES 1

1.
SERVE THE PASTA
REALE WITH LOTS
OF FRESHLY GRATED
PARMESAN.

2.
FOR ADULTS, STIR IN CHILLI,
CAYENNE PEPPER AND SPINACH
LEAVES. TOP WITH GRATED
PARMESAN AND SERVE.

Pad Thai with Chicken & Prawns

Not all my guys are into prawns and coriander for this dish...again feel free to assemble as you'd like.

INGREDIENTS
200 g (7 oz) packet dry rice noodles
2 tablespoons brown sugar
2½ tablespoons fish sauce
1½ tablespoons tomato sauce (ketchup)
3 teaspoons worcestershire sauce
2 tablespoons peanut oil
5 garlic cloves, crushed
450 g (1 lb) boneless, skinless chicken breasts, cut into 2 cm (¾ inch) cubes
2 eggs

180 g (6½ oz/2 cups) bean sprouts
4 spring onions (scallions), sliced
3 tablespoons chopped roasted peanuts
2 limes, cut into wedges

INGREDIENTS FOR ADULTS
1 teaspoon sambal oelek
250 g (9 oz) prawns (shrimp), shelled and deveined
½ cup chopped coriander (cilantro) leaves, loosely packed

METHOD
Prepare the noodles according to the packet instructions. Drain and set aside.

Combine the sugar, fish sauce, tomato sauce and worcestershire sauce, then divide into two small bowls.

1. **DISH ONE** Heat 1 tablespoon of peanut oil in a large frying pan or wok over a medium–high heat. Stir-fry half the garlic with half the chicken for 3 minutes. Add one bowl of the sauce mixture and cook for 2 minutes more. Lightly beat 1 egg then add it to the pan and stir constantly for 1 minute. Add half the rice noodles and toss until coated.

Stir in half the bean sprouts and spring onions and toss for 1 minute, or until heated through. Scatter over half the chopped peanuts and serve with wedges of lime for the kids to squeeze over the noodles.

2. **DISH TWO** Stir the sambal oelek through the remaining sauce mixture.

Heat the remaining peanut oil in a frying pan or wok over a medium–high heat. Stir-fry the remaining chicken and garlic for 3 minutes. Add the prawns and stir-fry for 2 minutes, or until the prawns turn pink. Pour in the sauce and cook for a further 2 minutes. Lightly beat the remaining egg then add it to the pan and cook for 1 minute, stirring constantly. Add the remaining rice noodles and toss to coat. Stir through the remaining bean sprouts and spring onions and half the coriander. Divide between the adults' plates. Scatter over the remaining chopped peanuts and coriander and garnish with wedges of lime.

SERVES 4

1.

RICE NOODLES WITH CHICKEN, EGG
AND BEAN SPROUTS FOR THE KIDS.

2.

ZINGY PAD THAI WITH PRAWNS,
SAMBAL OELEK AND FRESH
CORIANDER FOR ADULTS.

Tuna Meatballs with Parsley Pesto Pasta

The zesty, tangy, pesto hit makes these otherwise plain tuna meatballs adult-worthy. Serve the meatballs with Veggie spaghetti (page 77) if you'd rather skip the pasta. And if you like the idea of a sit-down family meal, cook the kids' and adults' meatballs at the same time in two separate pans.

INGREDIENTS
425 g (15 oz) tin tuna in oil, drained
100 g (3½ oz/1 cup) dry breadcrumbs
3 tablespoons pine nuts
grated zest of 1 lemon
1 egg
2 tablespoons olive oil,
    plus extra for drizzling
400 g (14 oz) spaghetti

INGREDIENTS FOR ADULTS
1 tablespoon chopped flat-leaf
    (Italian) parsley
2 teaspoons snipped chives

Parsley pesto
3 tablespoons blanched almonds
2 cups flat-leaf (Italian) parsley,
    loosely packed
⅓ cup snipped chives
80 ml (2½ fl oz/⅓ cup) olive oil
25 g (1 oz/¼ cup) grated parmesan
freshly ground black pepper

METHOD

Whiz the tuna, breadcrumbs, pine nuts, lemon zest and egg in a food processor until just combined. Halve the mixture.

Bring a large saucepan of salted water to the boil and cook the pasta according to the packet instructions. Reserve 250 ml (8½ fl oz/1 cup) of the cooking liquid and drain the pasta.

1. **DISH ONE** While the pasta is cooking, shape tablespoons of one portion of the tuna mixture into balls. Heat 1 tablespoon of the olive oil in a frying pan over a high heat and cook the tuna balls, turning frequently, for 2–3 minutes, or until nicely golden. To serve, drizzle a little olive oil over the pasta and top with the plain tuna meatballs.

2. **DISH TWO** To make the parsley pesto, pulse the almonds in a food processor until finely ground. Add the parsley, chives, olive oil and parmesan and pulse a little more. Season with pepper.

Mix the parsley and chives through the remaining tuna mixture and shape tablespoonfuls into balls. Heat the remaining olive oil in a frying pan over a high heat. Cook the tuna meatballs, turning frequently, for 2–3 minutes, or until golden. To serve, toss the pesto through the remaining pasta in a large bowl, adding a little of the reserved pasta cooking liquid to moisten. Top with the tuna meatballs and serve.

SERVES 4

Stuff on Stix & Stuff in Wraps

Anything on a stick is instantly more appealing to kids. Same as in a wrap or a bun. But for grown-ups it doesn't quite feel like a meal... SO just delete the stick or the 'wrap' when you want!

Moroccan Beef Kebabs with Couscous

For adults, there's spicy, Moroccan-flavoured tasty rump with fragrant couscous...for the kids, keep the couscous plain and serve with simple and juicy 'steak-and-veg on stix'. To save time, barbecue the kids' and adults' skewers at the same time.

INGREDIENTS

2 zucchini (courgettes), cut into 3 cm (1¼ inch) thick rounds
600 g (1 lb 5 oz) beef rump steak, trimmed, cut into 4 cm (1½ inch) cubes
1 onion, cut into wedges
185 g (6½ oz/1 cup) couscous
olive oil, for brushing
8 bamboo skewers, soaked for 30 minutes, or use metal skewers

INGREDIENTS FOR ADULTS

1 teaspoon finely grated lemon zest
2 teaspoons chopped mint
2 teaspoons chopped flat-leaf (Italian) parsley
1 teaspoon flaked almonds, toasted
1 teaspoon freshly grated nutmeg
1 teaspoon ground cumin
1 teaspoon ground coriander
¼ teaspoon ground allspice
¼ teaspoon ground ginger
pinch of cayenne pepper
pinch of ground cinnamon
1 tablespoon olive oil

METHOD

Preheat the grill of your barbecue to a medium heat.

Thread the zucchini, beef and onion alternately onto the skewers and divide onto two plates.

In a heatproof bowl, prepare the couscous according to the packet instructions. Fluff it up with a fork and divide into two portions.

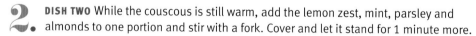

1. **DISH ONE** For the kids, lightly brush the skewers with olive oil, season with salt and grill for 3 minutes on each side for medium, or until cooked to their liking.

Keep the couscous plain and serve with the juicy beef skewers.

2. **DISH TWO** While the couscous is still warm, add the lemon zest, mint, parsley and almonds to one portion and stir with a fork. Cover and let it stand for 1 minute more.

In a bowl, combine the spices with the oil. Season with salt and brush the spicy mixture onto the adults' skewers. Barbecue for 3 minutes on each side for medium, or until cooked to your liking.

Remove the beef, onion and zucchini from the skewers and serve on the fragrant couscous.

SERVES 4

1.

SEASON THE KIDS'BEEF AND
ZUCCHINI SKEWERS WITH SALT
AND GRILL. SERVE THE JUICY 'STEAK
ON STIX' WITH PLAIN COUSCOUS.

2.

BRUSH THE BEEF WITH CUMIN,
CORIANDER AND HERBS FOR ADULTS.
SERVE ON A FRAGRANT MINT, LEMON
RIND AND ALMOND COUSCOUS.

Vietnamese Grilled Pork Meatballs

Kids can eat these meatballs straight from the skewer. Adults can slide them off and wrap them in lettuce leaves, along with slivers of cucumber, shredded carrots and fresh herbs. Serve them with a tangy nuoc cham dipping sauce.

INGREDIENTS

1 tablespoon fish sauce
2 teaspoons light soy sauce
1 large garlic clove, crushed
500 g (1 lb 2 oz) minced (ground) pork
peanut or vegetable oil, for brushing
steamed rice, to serve
8 bamboo skewers, soaked for 30 minutes

INGREDIENTS FOR ADULTS

4 iceberg lettuce leaves
½ telegraph (long) cucumber, halved
    lengthways and sliced on the diagonal
1 carrot, shredded
1 spring onion (scallion), sliced
small handful coriander (cilantro) leaves
small handful Vietnamese mint

Nuoc cham dipping sauce
1½ tablespoons fish sauce
1 tablespoon lime juice
1 tablespoon rice vinegar
½ teaspoon brown sugar
1–2 birdseye chillies, finely chopped
1 small garlic clove, crushed

METHOD

Combine the fish sauce, soy sauce and garlic in a bowl. Add the minced pork and mix with your hands. Form the mixture into 28 balls, each about 2 cm (¾ inch) in diameter. Thread the meatballs onto eight pre-soaked skewers – 3 meatballs per skewer for the kids and 4 meatballs per skewer for the adults. Refrigerate the skewers for 30 minutes to let them firm up.

Heat a barbecue grill or a frying pan to a medium–high heat.

Brush the meatballs with a little oil and cook them, turning frequently, for 6–8 minutes, or until browned on all sides and cooked through.

1. **DISH ONE** Serve the meatball sticks with plain rice for the kids.

2. **DISH TWO** To make the nuoc cham sauce, combine the ingredients with 1½ tablespoons of water in a small bowl. Serve the meatballs with the iceberg lettuce cups, cucumber, carrot, spring onion, coriander and mint, and the dipping sauce.

SERVES 4

Chicken Tikka Skewers with Cucumber Salad

I adore Indian food and the hotter the better, but the kids' tastebuds aren't quite ready for a vindaloo hit! They do however love the more subtle flavour of tandoori spices...which makes me happy!!

INGREDIENTS

2 tablespoons store-bought tandoori paste

250 g (9 oz/1 cup) Greek-style yoghurt

600 g (1 lb 5 oz) boneless, chicken thighs, cut into 3 cm (1¼ inch) pieces

olive oil spray

½ telegraph (long) cucumber, thinly sliced

INGREDIENTS FOR ADULTS

chopped coriander (cilantro) leaves, to serve

Raita

2 tablespoons Greek-style yoghurt

¼ telegraph (long) cucumber, seeded and finely chopped

½ tomato, seeded and finely chopped

few mint leaves, finely chopped

½ birdseye chilli, seeded and finely chopped

Cucumber salad

½ telegraph (long) cucumber, peeled and sliced

1 tablespoon white vinegar

½ birdseye chilli, seeded and finely chopped

METHOD

In a mixing bowl, combine the tandoori paste with the yoghurt. Mix the chicken pieces through the marinade until well coated. Cover with plastic wrap and refrigerate for 15 minutes to let the flavours infuse.

Preheat the oven to 180°C (350°F/Gas 4). Thread the chicken pieces onto eight skewers and place on a tray lined with baking paper. Spray the skewers lightly with olive oil. Bake for 10–12 minutes, or until cooked through.

1. DISH ONE Serve the kids' skewers with the sliced, plain cucumber.

2. DISH TWO To make the raita, combine all the ingredients in a bowl.

To make the cucumber salad, toss the cucumber, vinegar, chilli and ¼ cup of water in a bowl.

Remove the chicken from the skewers and sprinkle with the coriander. Serve with the raita and salad.

SERVES 4

SERVE THE KIDS' SKEWERS
WITH SLICED, PLAIN CUCUMBER.

COMBINE THE CUCUMBER, VINEGAR AND CHILLI.
REMOVE THE CHICKEN FROM THE SKEWERS,
SPRINKLE WITH CORIANDER AND SERVE WITH
THE CUCUMBER SALAD AND RAITA.

Barbecue Chicken Banh Mi

A different way to serve barbecue chicken...and it's so quick and easy. If I want to cut out the carb hit, I eat mine without the baguette.

INGREDIENTS

1 baguette

90 g (3 oz/⅓ cup) mayonnaise

1 barbecue chicken, skin removed and meat shredded

50 g (1½ oz) telegraph (long) cucumber, thinly sliced

50 g (1½ oz) grated carrot

INGREDIENTS FOR ADULTS

115 g (4 oz) grated carrot

100 g (3½ oz) grated daikon radish

130 g (4½ oz) telegraph (long) cucumber, thinly sliced

2 tablespoons rice vinegar

2 tablespoons sugar

½ teaspoon salt

coriander (cilantro) leaves, to serve

sliced pickled jalapeno chillies, to serve

lime wedges, to serve

METHOD

Cut the baguette into 4 equal portions.

1. **DISH ONE** For the kids' banh mi, slice a baguette portion in half lengthways then spread each half with ½ tablespoon of the mayonnaise. Add some chicken, cucumber slices and grated carrot and serve.

2. **DISH TWO** Toss together the carrot, daikon, cucumber, vinegar, sugar and salt in a bowl. Leave the vegetables to marinate at room temperature for at least 30 minutes then drain off the excess vinegar mixture.

   For the adults' banh mi, cut the baguettes in half lengthways and spread each half with ½ tablespoon of the mayonnaise. Add some shredded chicken, pickled vegetables, coriander leaves and jalapeno. Squeeze over some fresh lime and serve.

SERVES 4

Lemony Salmon Kebabs

The yummiest way for kids to enjoy salmon – barbecued on sticks with a squeeze of lemon. For the grown-ups, lemony salmon is dressed up with spicy salt. If you prefer to eat with your kids, you can prepare both versions of the skewers then cook them at the same time.

INGREDIENTS

700 g (1 lb 9 oz) salmon fillets, skinned and
    cut into 3 cm (1¼ inch) cubes
olive oil, for brushing
squeeze of lemon juice
salt
8 bamboo skewers, soaked for 30 minutes

INGREDIENTS FOR ADULTS

2 teaspoons oregano, chopped
2 teaspoons rosemary, chopped
1 teaspoon sesame seeds
½ teaspoon ground cumin
¼ teaspoon chilli flakes
½ teaspoon salt
1 tablespoon olive oil
1 lemon, very thinly sliced into rounds
crisp green salad, to serve

METHOD

Preheat a barbecue grill to medium or a frying pan over a medium heat.

Divide the salmon into two bowls.

1. **DISH ONE** Thread the salmon from one bowl onto four skewers. Lightly brush the salmon skewers with olive oil and sprinkle over a little lemon juice and salt.

Cook, turning occasionally, for 6–8 minutes, or until the fish is cooked through, and serve.

2. **DISH TWO** Combine the oregano, rosemary, sesame seeds, cumin, chilli flakes and salt in a small bowl.

Combine the olive oil and the salmon in a bowl. Add the spice mix and toss until the salmon is well coated. Thread a piece of fish then a slice of lemon, folded in half, onto a skewer and repeat until all the salmon and lemon is used up. (You should end up with four skewers.)

Cook the skewers, turning occasionally, for 6–8 minutes, or until the salmon is cooked through.

Serve the spicy lemony kebabs with a crisp green salad.

SERVES 4

Grilled Sausage Kebabs with Purple Slaw, Wasabi Mayo & Green Chilli

Thread cut snags onto sticks for the kids and for the adults, ditch the sticks and serve the sausages with a crunchy zingy wasabi slaw. You can prepare the kids' skewers first and fry them at the same time as the adults' snags.

INGREDIENTS
8 pork or beef sausages
125 g (4½ oz/½ cup) mayonnaise
125 g (4½ oz/½ cup) Greek-style yoghurt
squeeze of lemon juice
1 purple cabbage, shredded
4 bamboo skewers, soaked for 30 minutes

INGREDIENTS FOR ADULTS
2 teaspoons Greek-style yoghurt
wasabi paste, to taste
2 spring onions (scallions), finely shredded
small handful flat-leaf (Italian) parsley, chopped
1 green chilli, finely chopped
250 g (9 oz) mixed cherry tomatoes, halved
¼ red onion, finely chopped
olive oil, for drizzling
salt

METHOD
To make the slaw, combine the mayo, yoghurt and lemon juice in a large bowl. Toss the cabbage through the mayo mixture until well coated. Transfer half the slaw into another bowl.

 DISH ONE Preheat a frying pan over a medium heat.

Slice 4 sausages into 2 cm (¾ inch) thick discs and thread them onto the skewers. Cook the skewers, turning frequently, for 8–10 minutes, or until the sausages are browned and cooked through.

Serve to the kids with the plain purple slaw.

 DISH TWO Preheat a frying pan over a medium heat.

Meanwhile, combine the yoghurt and wasabi in a small bowl. Add the yoghurt mixture, spring onions and half the parsley to the remaining cabbage and toss. Top with the green chilli.

Mix the cherry tomatoes, red onion and remaining parsley in a bowl. Drizzle with olive oil and add salt to taste.

Fry the remaining sausages, turning often, for 8–10 minutes, or until they are cooked through. Serve with the spicy wasabi slaw and cherry tomato salad.

SERVES 4

Crispy Beef Lettuce Wraps

The classic Chinese dish, san choi bao, has always been a hit in our house – this tasty beef and pork version works a treat with, of course, the addition of fresh chilli and herbs for the adults.

INGREDIENTS
60 ml (2 fl oz/¼ cup) sunflower oil
250 g (9 oz) minced (ground) beef
250 g (9 oz) minced (ground) pork
salt
2 garlic cloves, crushed
4 cm (1½ inch) piece ginger, grated
1 tablespoon brown sugar
2 small cos (romaine) lettuces, separated into leaves
50 g (1½ oz) instant noodles, crumbled
For the dressing
2 teaspoons dark soy sauce
1 teaspoon light soy sauce
juice of ½ lime

2 teaspoons sesame oil
1 teaspoon fish sauce
1 teaspoon brown sugar
1 teaspoon light-flavoured olive oil

INGREDIENTS FOR ADULTS
1 tablespoon fish sauce
zest and juice of ½ lime
2 spring onions (scallions), chopped
1 small red chilli, finely chopped
2 tablespoons coriander (cilantro) leaves, chopped
2 tablespoons mint leaves, chopped
¼ red onion, thinly sliced

METHOD
Combine the dressing ingredients and separate into two bowls.

Heat two-thirds of the sunflower oil in a frying pan over a high heat. Combine the minced (ground) beef and pork, season with salt and fry for 5–7 minutes until well browned. Remove the meat from the pan and set aside.

Using the same pan, heat the remaining sunflower oil. Add the garlic, ginger, sugar and a pinch of salt and cook for 2 minutes over a medium heat. Return the meat to the pan and stir to combine well.

1. **DISH ONE** To serve the kids, scoop a little of the mince mixture into a lettuce leaf, drizzle with the dressing and top with some instant noodles.

2. **DISH TWO** To the remaining beef, add the fish sauce and stir for 1 minute. Add the lime zest and juice and mix well, then stir through the spring onion. Remove from the heat.

Add the chilli, coriander and mint to the dressing and stir. To serve, spoon some mince mixture into a lettuce leaf, add a splash of dressing and garnish with some red onion.

SERVES 4

1.

SCOOP A LITTLE OF THE FRIED MINCE
INTO A LETTUCE LEAF, DRIZZLE WITH
THE DRESSING AND TOP WITH SOME
INSTANT NOODLES.

2.

FOR THE ADULTS, ADD FISH SAUCE
TO THE MINCE AND CHILLI, CORIANDER
AND MINT TO THE DRESSING. SERVE IN
LETTUCE CUPS TOPPED WITH RED ONION.

Beef Sliders with Sweet Potato Chips

A different way to do 'burger and chips'. These are three-bite burgers...
kids eat them plain and adults can spice them up with onions, dill pickles
and hot chilli sauce.

INGREDIENTS
2 tablespoons vegetable oil
500 g (1 lb 2 oz) minced (ground) beef
8 small dinner rolls, cut in half
8 slices cheddar
salt and freshly ground black pepper
tomato sauce (ketchup), to serve
mustard, to serve
mayonnaise, to serve

Sweet potato chips
30 g (1 oz/½ cup) panko crumbs
1 teaspoon ground cumin

1 teaspoon sweet paprika
1 tablespoon olive oil
salt
1 large egg white
2 sweet potatoes, cut into
   1 cm (½ inch) sticks

INGREDIENTS FOR ADULTS
1 tablespoon vegetable oil
1 brown onion, sliced
dill pickles, to serve
hot chilli sauce

METHOD
Preheat the oven to 180°C (350°F/Gas 4).

For the chips, combine all the ingredients except the egg white and sweet potato
in a bowl. In a separate bowl, whisk the egg white until fluffy then add the sweet
potato. Mix through the panko crumbs until the chips are well coated. Spread out
on a baking tray lined with baking paper and cook for 10 minutes. Turn the chips and
cook for a further 15 minutes, or until the potato is tender and the crumbs crisp.

To prepare the burgers, divide the vegetable oil between two frying pans over a
medium–high heat. Form the mince into 8 equal-sized balls. Put 4 balls into each
pan and squish them down flat to form patties. Fry for 2 minutes, then flip. Add a slice
of cheese and the top of a bun to each patty. Cover the pan and cook for 2 minutes,
or until the cheese has melted.

1. **DISH ONE** Slide the kids' burgers out of the pan onto the bottom halves of the buns,
and serve with the sweet potato chips and condiments.

2. **DISH TWO** While the burgers are cooking, heat 1 tablespoon of oil in a frying pan over
a medium heat. Sauté the onion until nicely caramelised, about 3–4 minutes.

Assemble the adults' burgers and serve with the condiments, dill pickles, hot chilli
sauce and the caramelised onions.

SERVES 4

1.

SLIDE THE KIDS' BURGERS OUT
OF THE PAN ONTO THE BOTTOM
HALVES OF THE BUNS. SERVE
WITH SWEET POTATO CHIPS.

2.

FOR ADULTS, SERVE THE BURGERS
WITH CARAMELISED ONION, DILL
PICKLES, CHILLI SAUCE AND SWEET
POTATO CHIPS.

Roasted Pork & Prawn Crispy Pancakes

Light crispy coco-nutty pancakes with tasty pork and prawn for adults. Leave out the prawns and green bits for the kids.

INGREDIENTS

90 g (3 oz/½ cup) rice flour
125 ml (4 fl oz/½ cup) coconut milk
¼ teaspoon ground turmeric
½ teaspoon salt
1 tablespoon peanut oil, plus extra for frying
50 g (1½ oz/½ cup) bean sprouts
250 g (9 oz) Chinese barbecued pork (char sui), thinly sliced
1 iceberg lettuce, to serve
1 telegraph (long) cucumber, halved lengthways then sliced, to serve

INGREDIENTS FOR ADULTS

2 spring onions (scallions), sliced
coriander (cilantro) leaves, to serve
Vietnamese mint leaves, to serve

Prawn filling

250 g (9 oz) prawns (shrimp), shelled and deveined
2 teaspoons fish sauce
2 garlic cloves, crushed
¼ teaspoon salt
¼ teaspoon sugar
1 onion, thinly sliced

Nuoc cham dipping sauce

1 tablespoon lime juice
1½ tablespoons fish sauce
1 birdseye chilli, finely chopped
1 small garlic clove, crushed
1 tablespoon rice vinegar
½ teaspoon brown sugar

METHOD

In a mixing bowl, mix together the rice flour, coconut milk, ¾ cup of water, turmeric and salt to form a smooth batter. Leave to rest for 1 hour, or overnight if you have time.

To make the prawn filling, combine all of the ingredients except for the onion in a bowl. Cover and leave to marinate in the fridge for 30 minutes.

While the prawns are marinating, make the nuoc cham. Combine all of the ingredients with 1½ tablespoons of water in a small bowl and stir until the sugar has dissolved.

To finish the prawn filling, heat 1 tablespoon of peanut oil in a frying pan over a medium heat. Cook the onion until transluscent and add the prawns and their marinade. Cook until the prawns turn pink.

To cook the pancakes, heat a little oil in a non-stick frying pan over a medium–high heat. Pour in a thin layer of the pancake mixture and tilt the pan to swirl the batter over the base. Top with some bean sprouts, spring onions and a small handful of pork for the kids, or pork and prawns for the grown-ups. Cook for 5 minutes, or until the base is golden and crisp. (This is really important or the pancakes will fall apart!) Fold the pancake in half, slide onto a plate and keep warm. Repeat with the remaining pancake batter and filling.

Serve the pancakes on a large platter with the lettuce and cucumber for the kids, and the herbs and nuoc cham sauce for the grown-ups.

SERVES 4

Caesar Nachos

I love parmesan crisps; so do the kids. Make a heap and spread them on a plate 'nachos' style.

INGREDIENTS
60 g (2 oz/¼ cup) mayonnaise
2–3 teaspoons lemon juice
½ teaspoon dijon mustard
4 slices prosciutto or 4 thinly sliced
   bacon rashers
250 g (9 oz/2 ½ cups) grated parmesan
1 baby cos (romaine) lettuce, shredded
salt

INGREDIENTS FOR ADULTS
1 tablespoon olive oil
1 garlic clove, finely chopped
1 anchovy fillet in oil, finely chopped

METHOD
Preheat the oven to 200°C (400°/Gas 6).

To make the dressing, combine the mayonnaise, lemon juice and mustard and stir until smooth. Divide the dressing between two bowls.

To make the crispy prosciutto or bacon, heat a non-stick frying pan over a medium–high heat and add the prosciutto or bacon. Cook until golden, then leave to cool on paper towel to crisp up. Tear into pieces.

To make the parmesan crisps, line two baking trays with baking paper. On each tray, make 9 mounds of parmesan – use one tablespoon of parmesan per mound and leave several centimetres between them. Bake for 3–5 minutes until bubbly and golden. Remove from the oven and allow to cool and crisp up on the trays.

 DISH ONE Taste one of the bowls of dressing and adjust the seasoning to taste.

Arrange half the parmesan crisps on a platter and place a little lettuce on each crisp. Drizzle with the dressing and scatter over the crispy prosciutto or bacon.

 DISH TWO Heat the olive oil in a saucepan over a medium heat. Fry the chopped garlic until golden then drain on paper towel.

Stir the fried garlic and the anchovy through the remaining dressing.

Spread the remaining parmesan crisps on a platter and top each one with some lettuce and crispy prosciutto or bacon. Drizzle over the dressing and serve.

SERVES 4 AS A SNACK

1.
TOP THE PARMESAN CRISPS WITH
A LITTLE LETTUCE. DRIZZLE WITH
THE DRESSING AND SCATTER OVER
THE CRISPY BACON.

2.
STIR ANCHOVY AND FRIED GARLIC
THROUGH THE DRESSING. TOP THE
PARMESAN CRISPS WITH LETTUCE
AND CRISPY BACON, DRIZZLE OVER
THE DRESSING AND SERVE.

My Mexican Burritos

A mild and tasty wrap for the kids; for the adults, a spicy version served with salsa and plated up. Feel free to skip the tortilla if you want to avoid the boombah!

INGREDIENTS
1 tablespoon vegetable oil
1 onion, diced
4 garlic cloves, crushed
700 g (1 lb 9 oz) minced (ground) beef
1 teaspoon salt
400 g tin chopped tomatoes
6 corn tortillas
grated cheddar, to serve

INGREDIENTS FOR ADULTS
¾ teaspoon sweet paprika
1 teaspoon ground cumin
½ teaspoon ground coriander
½ teaspoon ground turmeric
1 birdseye chilli, chopped

Salsa
2 tomatoes, diced
½ red capsicum, seeded and diced
½ telegraph (long) cucumber, diced
3 spring onions (scallions), sliced
½ cup chopped coriander (cilantro) leaves
  and stems, loosely packed
1 small garlic clove, crushed
1 birdseye chilli, chopped
juice of ½ lime
1½ tablespoons olive oil
salt

METHOD
Heat the vegetable oil in a frying pan over a medium heat. Sauté the onion and garlic until translucent, about 2–3 minutes. Add the beef mince, season with salt and cook, stirring constantly, for about 5–7 minutes or until browned.

Transfer half the mince into another pan.

1. **DISH ONE** To one pan, add half the tinned tomatoes and ¼ cup of water, stir and bring to the boil. Reduce the heat to low–medium and cook for 25 minutes, stirring occasionally.

Heat the tortillas according to the packet instructions. Scoop some of the meat mixture into the tortillas, top with cheese and serve the burritos to the kids.

2. **DISH TWO** To the other pan, add the spices and chilli and cook over a medium heat for 1–2 minutes, or until the spices are fragrant. Add the remaining tinned tomatoes and ¼ cup of water, stir and bring to the boil. Reduce the heat to low–medium and cook for 25 minutes, stirring occasionally.

While the beef is cooking, combine the salsa ingredients in a bowl.

Serve the spicy beef with the fresh salsa for the grown-ups.

SERVES 4

1

SIMMER THE BEEF WITH ONION, GARLIC AND DICED TOMATOES. SERVE IN WARMED CORN TORTILLAS AND SPRINKLE WITH CHEESE.

2.

COOK THE BEEF WITH SPICES, CHILLI, ONION, GARLIC AND TOMATO. SERVE WITH A FRESH TOMATO, CORIANDER AND LIME SALSA.

Best Beef Fajitas

A great way to serve boring steak and veggies...

INGREDIENTS

¼ brown onion, finely chopped
1 garlic clove, crushed
½ teaspoon salt
½ teaspoon dried oregano
¼ teaspoon ground cumin
1½ tablespoons white wine vinegar
1½ tablespoons lime juice
1 tablespoon worcestershire sauce
1 tablespoon vegetable oil,
  plus extra for brushing
500 g (1 lb 2 oz) rump steak, thinly sliced
1 green capsicum (pepper), seeded
  and halved
1 red capsicum (pepper), seeded
  and halved
1 red onion, cut into wedges
6 corn tortillas
sour cream, to serve
grated cheddar, to serve

INGREDIENTS FOR ADULTS

Salsa
2 tomatoes chopped
1 small white onion, chopped
½ telegraph (long) cucumber, chopped
1 birdseye chilli, chopped
1 small green chilli, chopped
handful coriander (cilantro) leaves, chopped
juice of 1 lime
salt and freshly ground black pepper

Guacamole
1 ripe avocado
¼ red onion, very finely chopped
tabasco sauce, to taste
juice of ½ lime
1 teaspoon chilli flakes
handful coriander (cilantro), chopped
salt and freshly ground black pepper

METHOD

In a large bowl, combine the brown onion, garlic, salt, oregano, cumin, vinegar, lime juice, worcestershire sauce and 1 tablespoon of the vegetable oil. Toss the beef through the mixture. Cover and marinate – 4 hours is ripping, but 1 hour will do.

Preheat the grill of your barbecue to medium heat.

To make the salsa, combine all of the ingredients in a bowl. Add salt and pepper to taste.

To make the guacamole, mash the avocado with a fork until smooth. Stir in all of the other ingredients and add salt and pepper to taste.

Lightly brush the capsicums and red onion with oil. Cook the vegetables for 6–8 minutes per side, or until cooked through.

Drain the beef and discard the marinade. Cook the meat for 2–3 minutes, or until cooked.

Meanwile, warm the tortillas according to the packet instructions.

Transfer the beef to a plate and keep warm. Remove the vegetables to a chopping board. Cut the capsicums into bite-sized strips and separate the onion into pieces.

Arrange everything on a large platter so everyone can choose their own fillings. Serve with the tortillas and salsa, guacamole, sour cream and cheese.

SERVES 6

Chicken, Meat & Fish

I'm often stopped in the supermarket by mums and dads asking for inspiration for dinner ideas. So here's a bunch of meals that are easy and fast to prepare so you can turn your brain off!

Tuckshop Teriyaki Salmon

When necessity becomes a novelty! Wanted to cook fish in a bag...kids thought it hilarious I used their tuckshop lunch order bags. And so...

INGREDIENTS
2 × 150 g (5½ oz) skinless salmon fillets (for the adults)
2 × 100 g (3½ oz) skinless salmon fillets (for the kids)
1 tablespoon vegetable oil
salt
4 medium-sized paper bags
2 tablespoons good-quality teriyaki sauce
500 g (1 lb 2 oz) broccoli, cut into florets
steamed rice, to serve

INGREDIENTS FOR ADULTS
2 teaspoons rice vinegar
1 teaspoon sesame oil
2 teaspoons light-flavoured olive oil
1 teaspoon finely chopped ginger
1 teaspoon sesame seeds

METHOD
Preheat the oven to 180°C (350°F/Gas 4).

Wash the salmon under cold water and pat dry with paper towel. Rub half the vegetable oil over the salmon fillets and season one side of each with salt.

Heat a large frying pan over a medium–high heat and sear the salmon, salt-side down for about 1 minute. Season with more salt, turn and seal the other side.

Brush four squares of foil with the remaining oil. Place a salmon fillet onto each piece of foil. Turn up the edges of the foil to create a rim and drizzle each fillet with 2 teaspoons of teriyaki sauce.

Slide each foil tray with the fish into a paper bag. Sprinkle the outside of each bag with a little water. Seal each bag by tightly twisting the end and place on a baking tray. Cook in the oven for 15–20 minutes.

While the fish is baking, bring a saucepan of water to the boil. Put the broccoli into a steamer and cook, covered, over the boiling water for 3 minutes, or until the broccoli is just tender. Divide between two bowls.

Remove the fish from the oven.

 DISH ONE For the kids, serve the salmon with some steamed rice and plain broccoli.

 DISH TWO In a small bowl, combine the rice vinegar, sesame oil, olive oil, ginger and sesame seeds. Pour the mixture over the adults' broccoli and serve with the teriyaki salmon and steamed rice.

SERVES 4

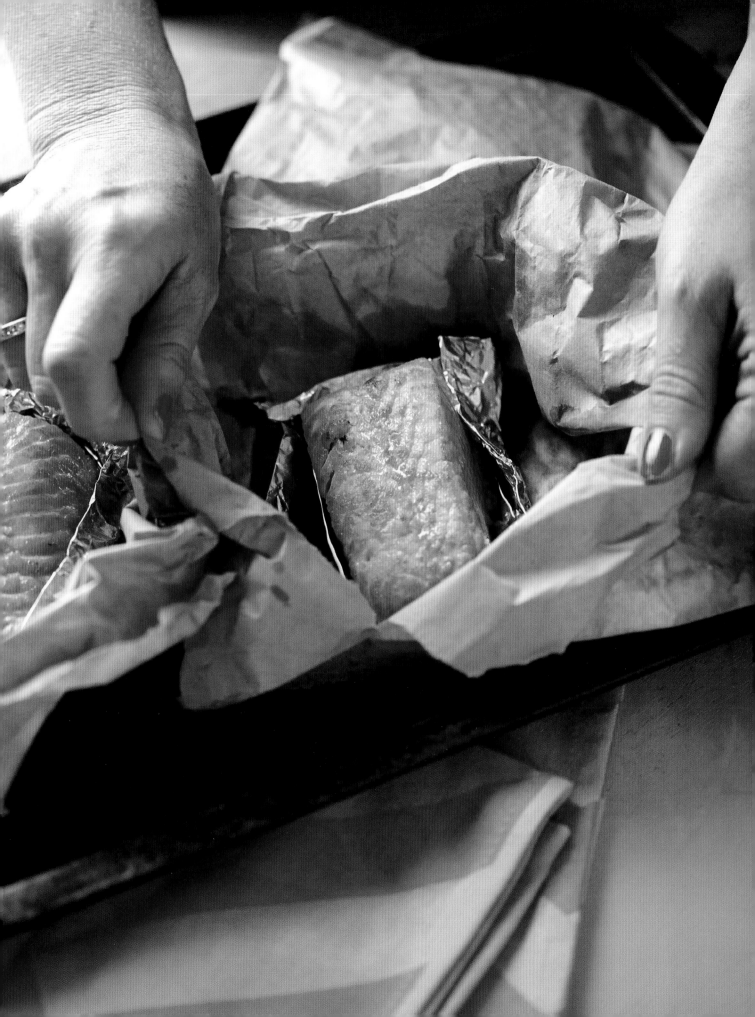

1.

FOR THE KIDS, SERVE
THE SALMON WITH SOME
STEAMED RICE AND PLAIN
BROCCOLI, IF DESIRED.

IN A SMALL BOWL, COMBINE THE RICE VINEGAR, SESAME OIL, OLIVE OIL, GINGER AND SESAME SEEDS. POUR THE MIXTURE OVER THE ADULTS' BROCCOLI AND SERVE WITH THE TERIYAKI SALMON AND STEAMED RICE.

Roasted Chicken with Carrots & Almonds

Sweet and sticky pan-roasted chicken and carrots with the licorishy lift of tarragon for the adults.

INGREDIENTS
12 baby carrots, peeled
3 tablespoons almonds, coarsely chopped
1 tablespoon honey
2 tablespoons olive oil
salt
4 chicken breasts on the bone, skin left on

INGREDIENTS FOR ADULTS
125 g (4½ oz/½ cup) Greek-style yoghurt
1 teaspoon grated lemon zest
freshly ground black pepper
½ shallot, finely chopped
1 tablespoon tarragon, chopped

METHOD
Preheat the oven to 190°C (375°F/Gas 5).

In a roasting tin, toss the carrots, almonds and honey with 1 tablespoon of the olive oil. Season with salt and roast for 20 minutes, or until the carrots are tender.

Meanwhile, heat the remaining oil in an ovenproof frying pan over a medium–high heat. Season the chicken and fry, skin side down, for 6–8 minutes, or until the skin is golden. Turn the chicken and transfer the pan to the oven. Bake for about 15 minutes, or until the chicken is cooked. Remove the chicken and carrots from the oven.

1. **DISH ONE** Serve out the kids' portions.

2. **DISH TWO** Mix together the yoghurt and lemon zest. Season well with salt and pepper.

Transfer the remaining chicken breasts to a plate and keep warm. Add the carrots, shallot and tarragon to the chicken pan and cook over a medium heat for 2–3 minutes.

Serve the adults' chicken with the lemony yoghurt and tarragon-coated carrots.

SERVES 4

Roasted Lamb with Hoisin Sauce

Slow-cooking lamb shoulder, basted in sticky hoisin sauce (yes from a jar), for four hours. Spice up for the adults with fresh chilli, peanuts and spring onions.

INGREDIENTS
60 ml (2 fl oz/¼ cup) tamari
60 ml (2 fl oz/¼ cup) light soy sauce
60 ml (2 fl oz/¼ cup) hoisin sauce
50 g (1½ oz/¼ cup) brown sugar
1 teaspoon Chinese five-spice
1 tablespoon sesame oil
3 cm (1¼ inch) piece ginger, finely grated
2 garlic cloves, crushed
60 ml (2 fl oz/¼ cup) rice wine
1.5 kg boned lamb shoulder
1 telegraph (long) cucumber, thinly sliced
steamed rice, to serve

INGREDIENTS FOR ADULTS
small handful mint, chopped
small handful coriander (cilantro) leaves, chopped
handful bean sprouts
2 spring onions (scallions), green part only, sliced
1 red chilli, sliced
3 tablespoons roasted salted peanuts, chopped

METHOD
Combine the tamari, soy sauce, hoisin sauce, sugar, five-spice, sesame oil, ginger, garlic and 2 tablespoons of the rice wine in a large zip-lock bag. Put the lamb in the bag and coat well with the mixture then leave it to marinate for 3 hours in the fridge.

Preheat the oven to 160°C (320°F/Gas 3). Drain the lamb and reserve the marinade. Put the lamb in a roasting tin, cover it with foil and roast for 1½ hours. Increase the heat to 180°C (350°F/Gas 4), remove the foil and cook for a further 30 minutes, or until tender and a bit crispy. Transfer the lamb to a plate, cover and let stand for 10 minutes.

Meanwhile, bring the reserved marinade to the boil in a small saucepan over a medium–high heat. Reduce the heat to low and simmer uncovered until it has thickened slightly, about 5 minutes. Strain and keep warm.

Toss the cucumber in a bowl with the remaining rice wine and divide into two bowls.

Slice the lamb and drizzle with the sauce.

1. **DISH ONE** Serve the kids slices of lamb with some cucumber and steamed rice.

2. **DISH TWO** Toss the mint, coriander and bean sprouts through the remaining cucumber. Scatter the spring onion, chilli and peanuts over the grown-ups' lamb and serve with the salad and steamed rice.

SERVES 4

Coco-Nutty Chicken Wings

Wings are the perfect size for little kids...I prefer the ribs as they seem to have more meat. These are great with Sweet potato chips (page 110), or served as finger food at grown-up parties. After marinating the wings, you can bake both versions at the same time.

INGREDIENTS

60 ml (2 fl oz/¼ cup) vegetable oil

2 tablespoons dark soy sauce

2 tablespoons honey

½ teaspoon salt

½ teaspoon grated lemon zest

250 ml (8½ fl oz/1 cup) coconut milk

500 g (1 lb 2 oz) chicken wings, halved at the joint, or 800 g (1 lb 12 oz) chicken ribs

3 tablespoons flaked coconut, toasted

INGREDIENTS FOR ADULTS

½ teaspoon curry powder

¼ teaspoon freshly ground black pepper

Asian slaw

1 teaspoon sesame oil

1 tablespoon olive oil

1 teaspoon light soy sauce

squeeze of lemon juice

100 g (3½ oz) bag store-bought coleslaw, without dressing

METHOD

In a large bowl, combine the vegetable oil, soy sauce, honey, salt and lemon zest. Whisk in the coconut milk. Divide between two bowls.

1. **DISH ONE** Scoop out ¼ cup of the marinade from one bowl and set aside. Put half the chicken into the same bowl and coat with the marinade. Cover and refrigerate for 1 hour – or, if you're really organised, overnight.

Preheat the oven to 140°C (275°F/Gas 1). Transfer the wings to a baking tray and cook for 5–6 minutes per side, or until the chicken is cooked through.

Meanwhile, heat the reserved marinade in a small saucepan over a medium heat until warmed through. To serve, drizzle the marinade over the chicken and scatter over the coconut.

2. **DISH TWO** To the other bowl of marinade, whisk in the curry powder and pepper then reserve ¼ cup of the marinade. Add the remaining chicken to the bowl and coat well with the marinade. Cover and refrigerate for 1 hour – or, overnight if you have time.

Preheat the oven to 140°C (275°F/Gas 1). Transfer the wings to a baking tray and cook for 5–6 minutes per side, or until the chicken is cooked through.

In a bowl, combine the sesame and olive oils, soy sauce and lemon juice to make the Asian slaw dressing. Toss the coleslaw through the dressing.

Meanwhile, warm the reserved marinade in a small saucepan over a medium heat until warmed through. To finish, drizzle the marinade over the chicken and scatter over the coconut. Serve with the Asian slaw on the side.

SERVES 6 AS PART OF A MAIN COURSE

1

MARINATE THE CHICKEN IN SOY,
HONEY, LEMON ZEST AND COCONUT
MILK. BAKE IN THE OVEN AND SERVE
WITH TOASTED COCONUT FLAKES.

2.

FOR THE ADULTS, ADD CURRY
POWDER AND PEPPER TO THE
MARINADE. BAKE AND SERVE
WITH A CRISP ASIAN SLAW.

Inside-Out Chicken Pie

I've said before how much I love pies…but they don't love my bottom. The kids can still enjoy this inside-out version. Serve theirs with pastry, but if you're feeling in the mood for something lighter, just have the mixture with the beans and a little butter. I also 'cheat' and use a barbecue chook, but of course this would taste better with the real deal.

INGREDIENTS

1 × 165 g (6 oz) sheet store-bought puff pastry, thawed
420 g (15 oz) tin cream of chicken soup
250 ml (8½ fl oz/1 cup) milk
350 g (12½ oz) shredded barbecue chicken
200 g (7 oz) frozen peas, corn and carrots
⅛ teaspoon salt
⅛ teaspoon garlic powder

INGREDIENTS FOR ADULTS

1 teaspoon thyme
¼ teaspoon cajun spice mix
freshly ground black pepper
100 g (3½ oz) green beans, steamed
butter, to serve

METHOD

Preheat the oven to 200°C (400°F/Gas 6).

Unfold the pastry on a lightly floured surface and cut into 4 squares. Using a fork, pierce each square a few times. Put the sqaures on an ungreased baking tray.

Bake for about 15 minutes, or until golden brown. Remove from the oven and set aside.

While the pastry is baking, combine the soup and milk in a large bowl.

Heat a large frying pan over a medium heat. Add the soup mixture, shredded chicken, vegetables, salt and garlic powder and cook, stirring frequently, for about 5 minutes, or until the mixture is hot. Divide the mixture in two.

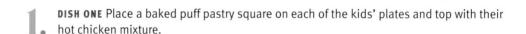

1. **DISH ONE** Place a baked puff pastry square on each of the kids' plates and top with their hot chicken mixture.

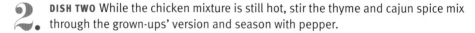

2. **DISH TWO** While the chicken mixture is still hot, stir the thyme and cajun spice mix through the grown-ups' version and season with pepper.

Spoon the chicken over the puff pastry and serve with green beans topped with butter.

SERVES 4

Pretzel-Crusted Chicken

Crushed up pretzels. Coating chicken. Then baked. I'm not kidding.
Crispy, salty, yummmy. It's perfect with steamed green beans.

INGREDIENTS
200 g (7 oz) pretzels, coarsely crushed
1 egg, beaten
1 tablespoon milk
4 skinless, boneless chicken breasts

INGREDIENTS FOR ADULTS
½ teaspoon dried thyme
125 ml (4 fl oz/½ cup) vegetable oil
60 g (2 oz/¼ cup) wholegrain mustard
1 tablespoon dijon mustard
1½ tablespoons red wine vinegar
salt and freshly ground black pepper

METHOD
Preheat the oven to 180°C (350°F/Gas 4).

Blitz the crushed pretzels in a food processor until you have a mixture of coarse and fine crumbs. Divide the crumbs between two plates.

1. **DISH ONE** In a shallow bowl, whisk together the egg and the milk. Dip a chicken breast in the egg mixture then coat with the pretzel crumbs. Put the chicken on a baking tray lined with baking paper. Repeat with another chicken breast.

Bake for 20–25 minutes, or until cooked through. Slice the chicken and serve.

2. **DISH TWO** Mix the thyme through the remaining pretzel crumbs.

Combine the vegetable oil, mustards, vinegar and 1½ tablespoons of water in a food processor until smooth. Season with salt and pepper.

Pour half of the dressing into a shallow bowl. Dip a chicken breast in the dressing, then coat with the pretzel crumbs. Transfer to a baking tray lined with baking paper. Repeat with the remaining chicken breast.

Bake in the oven for 20–25 minutes, or until cooked through. Slice the chicken and serve with the reserved dressing.

SERVES 4

Apricotty Lamb Tagine

Sweet apricots, dates and fragrant butternut pumpkin make this a delicious Middle Eastern family meal.

INGREDIENTS
60 ml (2 fl oz/¼ cup) olive oil
1 onion, finely diced
2 small carrots, finely diced
600 g (1 lb 5 oz) diced lamb
2 garlic cloves, crushed
1 teaspoon ground cumin
½ teaspoon ground ginger
¼ teaspoon saffron threads
½ cinnamon stick
¼ teaspoon ground allspice
1 tablespoon honey
80 g (2¾ oz) dried apricots, cut into quarters
2 stoned dates, cut into quarters
1 vegetable stock cube

1 small butternut pumpkin (squash), cut into 2 cm (¾ inch) cubes
squeeze of lemon juice
salt and freshly ground black pepper
185 g (6½ oz/1 cup) dry couscous

INGREDIENTS FOR ADULTS
2 tablespoons chopped flat-leaf (Italian) parsley
2 tablespoons chopped coriander (cilantro) leaves, plus extra to serve
2 tablespoons toasted pine nuts
grated zest of ½ orange
¼ teaspoon ground chilli
chopped red chilli, to serve

METHOD

Heat 2 tablespoons of the olive oil in a heavy-based saucepan over a medium heat. Cook the onion and carrot for 3–4 minutes, or until the vegetables have softened.

Add the lamb and brown all over. Stir in the garlic, cumin, ginger, saffron, cinnamon stick and allspice and cook for 2 minutes. Add the honey, apricots and dates, crumble in the stock cube and pour in enough boiling water to cover the meat – about 2 cups (500 ml/12 fl oz). Stir and bring to the boil. Lower the heat, cover and simmer gently for 45 minutes.

Remove the lid and cook for a further 30 minutes. Stir in the pumpkin and simmer for 20–30 minutes more, or until the pumpkin and lamb are tender.

Meanwhile, prepare the couscous according to the packet instructions. Add the remaining olive oil, the lemon juice and salt and pepper to the couscous and combine.

 DISH ONE Serve out some couscous onto the kids' plates and top with the tagine.

 DISH TWO Stir the parsley, coriander, pine nuts and orange zest through the remaining couscous. Stir the ground chilli through the tagine and serve on a bed of couscous. Garnish with the fresh chilli and coriander.

SERVES 6

1.
SERVE OUT SOME COUSCOUS ONTO THE KIDS' PLATES AND TOP WITH THE TAGINE.

2.
STIR THE PARSLEY, CORIANDER, PINE NUTS AND ORANGE ZEST THROUGH THE COUSCOUS. ADD THE CHILLI TO THE TAGINE AND SERVE.

Moroccan Mini Meatloaves

Simply make up the meatloaf filling...I can't quite bear the thought of eating these as cupcakes and prefer to bake mine in a small meatloaf dish. But the kids think the cupcakes are brilliant.

INGREDIENTS

500 g (1 lb 2 oz) minced (ground) lamb
1 tablespoon tomato sauce (ketchup)
1 tablespoon honey
55 g (2 oz/½ cup) almond meal
1 egg, lightly beaten
1¼ teaspoons salt
3 potatoes, peeled and diced
2 tablespoons butter
2 tablespoons milk
30 g (1 oz/¼ cup) grated cheddar

INGREDIENTS FOR ADULTS

½ red onion, finely chopped
1 garlic clove, crushed
¼ teaspoon ground cumin
¼ teaspoon ground coriander
¼ teaspoon ground chilli
¼ teaspoon ras el hanout
½ cup coriander (cilantro) leaves, roughly chopped
3 tablespoons toasted pine nuts
freshly ground black pepper

Cauliflower topping
½ cauliflower, cut into florets
1 tablespoon milk
1 tablespoon Greek-style yoghurt
1 teaspoon prepared horseradish
salt and freshly ground black pepper

METHOD

Preheat the oven to 180°C (350°F/Gas 4).

Combine the lamb, tomato sauce, honey, almond meal, egg and 1 teaspoon of the salt in a bowl. Remove half the mixture to a separate bowl and set aside.

1.

DISH ONE Lightly oil a standard 6-hole muffin tin. Divide one portion of the meat mixture into 6 equal-sized balls and press them into the muffin holes. Bake in the oven for 30–35 minutes, or until the lamb is cooked through.

Meanwhile, bring a saucepan of salted water to the boil. Cook the potatoes until they are soft, about 15 minutes.

Drain the potatoes and mash them until smooth. Add the butter, milk, remaining salt and half the cheese and combine.

When the mini meatloaves are cooked, remove them from the oven and top with the mash. Increase the oven temperature to 230°C (450°F/Gas 8) and bake the meatloaves for around 5–6 minutes, or until the mash develops a golden brown crust.

Allow them to cool for a few minutes then serve to the kids.

2. **DISH TWO** To the remaining mince mixture, add the onion, garlic, spices, fresh coriander and pine nuts. Season with salt and pepper and mix well. Divide the mixture between two 9.5 cm × 7.5 cm (3¾ × 3 inch) (350 ml/12 fl oz) mini loaf tins or press into a lightly oiled standard 6-hole muffin tin. Bake for 40–45 minutes (or 30–35 minutes if cooking in the muffin tins), or until the meatloaves are cooked through.

Meanwhile, prepare the cauliflower topping. Microwave the cauliflower and milk in a microwave-safe dish for about 5–6 minutes, or until the cauliflower is tender. Add the remaining cheese, the yoghurt, horseradish and salt and pepper, and whiz in a food processor until it resembles mashed potato.

When the meatloaves are ready, remove them from the oven and top with the mash. Increase the heat to 230°C (450°F/Gas 8) and bake for 5–6 minutes more, or until the mash is golden brown. Allow them to cool for a few minutes and serve to the adults.

SERVES 4

1.

BAKE LAMB MINI MEATLOAF MUFFINS
TOPPED WITH CREAMY MASHED
POTATO FOR THE KIDS.

2.

ADD MOROCCAN SPICES, ONION, GARLIC
AND PINE NUTS FOR ADULTS AND TOP
WITH CAULIFLOWER MASH.

Soy Chicken with Soba Noodles

A delicious soothing chickeny and slippery noodley dish served with added herbs and spices for the grown-ups.

INGREDIENTS

80 ml (2½ fl oz/⅓ cup) soy sauce
2 tablespoons mirin
2 tablespoons rice vinegar
4 boneless, skinless chicken thighs, cut in half
1 tablespoon vegetable oil
270 g (9½ oz) soba noodles

INGREDIENTS FOR ADULTS

2 tablespoons sliced pickled ginger
1 teaspoon sesame oil
1 spring onion (scallion), thinly sliced
chopped red chilli, to serve
small handful coriander (cilantro) leaves

METHOD

In a mixing bowl, combine the soy, mirin and rice vinegar. Add the chicken and mix with the marinade. Cover with plastic wrap and refrigerate for 15–20 minutes. (Even 10 will do.)

Heat the vegetable oil in a frying pan over a medium–high heat.

Drain the chicken and reserve the marinade. Cook the chicken for about 4 minutes on each side, or until cooked through.

Cook the noodles according to the packet instructions, then drain. Divide the noodles between four serving bowls.

Bring the reserved marinade to the boil in a small saucepan and simmer over a medium heat for 2–3 minutes, or until thickened. Pour the sauce into a jug and keep warm until ready to serve.

1. **DISH ONE** For the kids, keep the noodles plain. Top with some soy chicken and let the kids help themselves to the sauce.

2. **DISH TWO** Add the pickled ginger, sesame oil, spring onion, chilli and coriander to the adults' noodles. Top with the remaining soy chicken and serve with the sauce.

SERVES 4

Roasted Chicken with Lemon *(inspired by Yotam Ottolenghi)*

Ottolenghi is one of my favourite cookbook authors. If you can't find Jerusalem artichokes, use kipfler potatoes.

INGREDIENTS

450 g Jerusalem artichokes, peeled, cut into 2 cm (¾ inch) thick wedges

2 tablespoons lemon juice

8 chicken thighs, on the bone and skin left on, or a medium whole chicken, divided into four

12 shallots, halved lengthways

12 large garlic cloves, sliced

1 lemon, halved lengthways and thinly sliced

1 teaspoon saffron threads

2½ tablespoons olive oil

1 tablespoon pink peppercorns, slightly crushed

5 thyme sprigs

1 tablespoon chopped tarragon leaves

2 teaspoons salt

INGREDIENTS FOR ADULTS

1 tablespoon chopped tarragon leaves

1 tablespoon lemon juice

8 green olives (optional)

freshly ground black pepper

METHOD

In a saucepan, cover the Jerusalem artichokes with water, add the lemon juice and bring to the boil over a high heat. Lower the heat and simmer for about 10 minutes, or until the artichokes are just tender. Drain and allow to cool.

Combine the artichokes and all the remaining ingredients in a large mixing bowl until the chicken is well coated. Cover and leave to marinate in the fridge for 2 hours, or overnight if you're really organised.

Preheat the oven to 240°C.

Put the chicken, skin side up, in the centre of a roasting tin and scatter the remaining ingredients around the chicken pieces. Roast for 30 minutes. Cover the tin with foil and cook for a further 15 minutes, or until the chicken is cooked. Remove from the oven.

 DISH ONE Serve out some of the chicken and veggies onto the kids' plates.

 DISH TWO To the remaining chicken and vegetables, add the tarragon, lemon juice, green olives (if using) and plenty of freshly ground black pepper. Combine in the roasting tin then serve immediately.

SERVES 4

1.
SERVE OUT SOME OF THE CHICKEN AND VEGGIES ONTO THE KIDS' PLATES.

2.
TO THE REMAINING CHICKEN, ADD THE TARRAGON, LEMON JUICE, GREEN OLIVES AND PLENTY OF FRESHLY GROUND BLACK PEPPER. MIX WELL AND SERVE IMMEDIATELY.

Spicy Cumin Lamb Ribs

(inspired by Dainty Sichuan)

I'm sure you've gathered by now I'm a massive chilli head. My kids, on the other hand, are not chilli heads. This dish is an attempt to recreate one of my favourite dishes at the insanely delicious Melbourne restaurant Dainty Sichuan. Clearly I cook this dish in two batches.

INGREDIENTS

2 tablespoons vegetable oil, plus more for frying
1 kg (2 lb 3 oz) lamb ribs (or cutlets)
100 ml (3½ fl oz) light soy sauce
100 ml (3½ fl oz) kecap manis
800 ml (27 fl oz) chicken stock
3 cm (1¼ inch) piece ginger, roughly chopped
5 garlic cloves, roughly chopped
2 egg whites, lightly beaten
1 tablespoon plain (all-purpose) flour

INGREDIENTS FOR ADULTS

2 teaspoons salt
1 tablespoon chilli powder
1 tablespoon cumin seeds, coarsely ground
1 tablespoon coriander seeds, coarsely ground
2 teaspoons garlic powder
pinch of chilli flakes
1 small red chilli, chopped
1 spring onion (scallion), chopped
small handful coriander (cilantro) leaves
1 tablespoon unsalted peanuts, toasted

METHOD

Preheat the oven to 180°C (350°F/Gas 4).

Heat the vegetable oil in a large frying pan over a high heat and brown the lamb on both sides. Transfer to a roasting tin and add the soy sauce, kecap manis, stock, ginger and garlic. Coat the lamb in the marinade, cover the tin with foil and bake for 3½ hours.

Remove the lamb from the tin and allow it to cool.

When ready to finish and serve the dish, cut the lamb into individual ribs. Coat the lamb in the egg whites and divide between two bowls.

1. **DISH ONE** Sprinkle the flour over one bowl of lamb and mix.

Heat some oil in a large frying pan or wok over a medium–high heat. Working in batches, fry the lamb for 2 minutes per batch and drain on paper towel.

Serve the plain, crispy lamb ribs to the kids.

2. **DISH TWO** Add the salt, chilli powder, cumin seeds, coriander seeds and garlic powder to the other bowl of lamb and combine.

Again working in batches, cook the spicy lamb in the frying pan or wok for 2 minutes and drain on paper towel.

Serve the spicy ribs topped with the chilli flakes, fresh chilli, spring onion, fresh coriander and peanuts.

SERVES 4

Chicken Kiev

I love the traditional version, but this turns the chicken inside out... the 'crumbs' are actually almond meal and the butter is mixed into the 'crumbs'. Leave out the parsley if your little guys don't like the green bits...

INGREDIENTS

100 g (3½ oz/1 cup) almond meal
3 garlic cloves, crushed
salt
50 g (1¾ oz) butter, melted
4 boneless, skinless chicken breasts, pounded flat

Apple and beetroot salad
4 beetroot (beets)
olive oil, for drizzling
4 thyme sprigs
salt
1 green apple, thinly sliced

INGREDIENTS FOR ADULTS

2 tablespoons finely chopped flat-leaf (Italian) parsley

Apple and beetroot salad dressing
2 tablespoons apple cider vinegar
½ teaspoon dijon mustard
60 ml (2 fl oz/¼ cup) olive oil
1½ tablespoons prepared horseradish
salt and freshly ground black pepper
3 tablespoons salted pistachios, chopped

METHOD

Preheat the oven to 180°C (350°F/Gas 4).

In a roasting tin, drizzle the beetroot with olive oil, scatter over the thyme and season with salt. Cover with foil and roast for about 1½ hours, or until the beetroot is cooked.

Meanwhile, combine the almond meal, garlic and salt in a bowl.

When the beetroot is tender, remove them from the oven and let them cool. Peel and cut the beetroot into thin wedges. Divide the beetroot between two bowls and add half the apple to each.

1. **DISH ONE** Cut 2 chicken breasts into 'nuggets'. Brush with butter and coat in the almond mixture. Bake the chicken on a baking tray lined with baking paper for 15–20 minutes, or until the crumbing is golden and the chicken is cooked through.

Add a little salt and olive oil to one bowl of beetroot and apple. Serve with the chicken kiev 'nuggets'.

2. **DISH TWO** Mix the parsley through the remaining almond mixture. Brush the remaining chicken with butter and press the almond mixture onto the chicken. Bake the chicken on a baking tray lined with baking paper for 15–20 minutes, or until cooked through.

Meanwhile, make the salad dressing. Whisk together the vinegar and mustard in a bowl. Whisk in the olive oil until combined then stir in the horseradish and season with salt and pepper. Drizzle the dressing onto the beetroot and apple salad and sprinkle with the pistachios. Serve with the adults' chicken kiev.

SERVES 4

1.

CRUMB BITE-SIZED CHICKEN PIECES
IN ALMOND MEAL TO MAKE CHICKEN
KIEV 'NUGGESTS' FOR THE KIDS.
SERVE WITH BEETROOT AND APPLE.

FOR ADULTS, ADD PARSLEY TO THE
CRUMBING AND SERVE CRISPY 'INSIDE-
OUT' CHICKEN KIEV WITH A BEETROOT,
APPLE AND PISTACHIO SALAD.

Pork Tonkatsu

We call this Japanese schnitzel because that's basically what it is! The kids can have it sushi-sandwich-style, between slices of fresh white bread; the grown-ups can have it on cabbage with a tasty spicy sauce.

INGREDIENTS
4 boneless pork loin steaks
salt and freshly ground black pepper
75 g (2¾ oz/½ cup) plain (all-purpose) flour
2 eggs, beaten
120 g (4½ oz/2 cups) panko crumbs
vegetable oil, for frying
4 slices of white bread

INGREDIENTS FOR ADULTS
150 g (5½ oz) shredded cabbage
lemon wedges, to serve

Tonkatsu sauce
1 tablespoon tomato sauce (ketchup)
1½ teaspoons soy sauce
1 teaspoon mustard powder
½ teaspoon ground allspice

Cabbage dressing
½ garlic clove, crushed
½ teaspoon sesame oil
1 tablespoon mirin
2 teaspoons white miso paste
1 tablespoon rice vinegar

METHOD
Season both sides of the pork loins with salt and pepper. Coat the loins with the flour, dip them in the egg and cover well with the panko crumbs.

Heat the vegetable oil in a frying pan over a high heat.

1. DISH ONE Shallow-fry 2 pork loins for about 3–4 minutes on each side, or until they are golden brown. Drain on paper towel and slice up into bite-sized pieces. Serve between slices of fresh white bread.

2. DISH TWO To make the tonkatsu sauce, combine the tomato sauce, soy sauce, mustard powder and allspice in a small bowl.

To make the cabbage dressing, mix together the garlic, sesame oil, mirin, miso paste and rice vinegar in another small bowl and set aside.

Shallow-fry the remaining pork for about 3–4 minutes on each side, or until golden brown. Drain on paper towel and slice.

Arrange the cabbage and pork on the adults' plates, and garnish with wedges of lemon. Serve with the tonkatsu sauce and cabbage dressing.

SERVES 4

Chicken Satay with Hokkien Noodles

An oldie but a goodie...The sauce is quite mild so you'll need to pump up the flavour for the grown-ups with the additon of some fresh chopped chilli if you like. I also ditch the noodles for my trusty Cauliflower 'rice' and add a salad on the side!

INGREDIENTS

1 tablespoon peanut oil

1 onion, sliced

2 garlic cloves, crushed

1 teaspoon grated ginger

500 g (1 lb 2 oz) boneless, skinless chicken breasts, cut into cubes

½ green capsicum (pepper), seeded and sliced

100 g (3½ oz) green beans, cut into 3 cm (1¼ inch) lengths

1 carrot, diced

2 tablespoons sweet chilli sauce

2 tablespoons dark soy sauce

2 tablespoons crunchy peanut butter

1 tablespoon rice vinegar

200 g (7 oz) hokkien noodles

INGREDIENTS FOR ADULTS

2 handfuls green salad leaves

½ teaspoon sesame oil

1 teaspoon olive oil

squeeze of lemon juice

salt and freshly ground black pepper

1 quantity Cauliflower 'rice' (page 20)

METHOD

Heat the peanut oil in a large wok over a high heat. Sauté the onion, garlic and ginger until the onion begins to soften, about 3 minutes. Add the chicken and stir-fry for about 4–5 minutes, or until the chicken starts to brown. Add the capsicum, beans and carrot, and fry for a further 5 minutes, or until the vegetables and chicken are cooked through.

Add the sweet chilli and soy sauces, peanut butter, rice vinegar and ¼ cup of water to the wok and stir.

Remove half the chicken mixture to a bowl and keep warm.

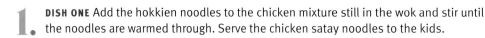

1. **DISH ONE** Add the hokkien noodles to the chicken mixture still in the wok and stir until the noodles are warmed through. Serve the chicken satay noodles to the kids.

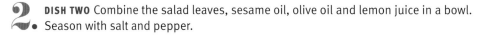

2. **DISH TWO** Combine the salad leaves, sesame oil, olive oil and lemon juice in a bowl. Season with salt and pepper.

Serve the remaining chicken with the salad and Cauliflower 'Rice'.

SERVES 4

2.

COMBINE THE SALAD LEAVES,
SESAME OIL, OLIVE OIL AND LEMON
JUICE. SERVE WITH THE CHICKEN
SATAY AND CAULIFLOWER 'RICE'.

1.

STIR THE HOKKIEN NOODLES
THROUGH THE CHICKEN SATAY
AND SERVE.

Steak with Spicy Salt

This steak has a tasty Mexican vibe...the coating is crunchy and spicy and has a real chilli hit. The Mamasita corn (page 194) is a ripping accompaniment to go with this dish.

INGREDIENTS

2 × 150 g (5½ oz) porterhouse steaks (for the adults)

2 × 100 g (3½ oz) porterhouse steaks (for the kids)

olive oil, for brushing

salt

1 carrot, cut into sticks

½ telegraph (long) cucumber, cut into sticks

2 celery stalks, cut into sticks

Homemade potato fries

500 g (1 lb 2 oz) potatoes, peeled and cut into 1 cm (½ inch) thick chips

2 tablespoons olive oil

salt

INGREDIENTS FOR ADULTS

2 teaspoons salt

2 teaspoons coriander seeds

2 teaspoons black peppercorns

1 teaspoon hot paprika

1 teaspoon chilli flakes

½ teaspoon dill seeds

1 garlic clove, crushed

250 g (9 oz) small tomatoes, halved

250 g zucchini, cut into strips

METHOD

Preheat the oven to 120°C (250°F/Gas ½). Line a baking tray with foil. Spread the salt, coriander seeds, peppercorns, paprika, chilli flakes, dill seeds and garlic on the baking tray, and roast for about 30 minutes, or until the garlic is dry. Using a mortar and pestle or spice grinder crush the spice mix until coarsely ground.

Remove the steaks from the fridge 30 minutes before cooking. Sprinkle the adults' steaks with the spice mix. Cover all the steaks with plastic wrap and set aside.

Increase the oven temperature to 220°C (430°F/Gas 7) for the potato fries. To prepare the potato fries, arrange the chips in a single layer on a baking tray lined with baking paper. Drizzle with the olive oil and season with salt. Bake for 10 minutes then turn the chips and reduce the heat to 200°C (400°F/Gas 6). Continue baking for another 30–35 minutes, turning every 10 minutes, and remove from the oven when the chips are crisp, golden and cooked through.

Heat a heavy-based frying pan over a high heat until it's searing hot.

1. **DISH ONE** Cook the plain steaks for 3 minutes on each side, or until cooked to the kids' liking.

Rest the steaks for 5 minutes, then serve with some of the potato fries and the veggie sticks.

2. **DISH TWO** Return the frying pan to the heat. When it's searing hot, add the steaks and cook for 3 minutes on each side, or until cooked to your liking. Remove the steaks to a chopping board and let them rest for 5–10 minutes.

Meanwhile, heat a chargrill pan over a medium–high heat. Brush the tomatoes and zucchinis lightly with oil and grill, turning occasionally, for about 5 minutes or until nicely marked and cooked through.

Slice the rested steaks and serve with the grilled veggies and the potato fries.

SERVES 4

1.

COOK THE PLAIN STEAKS AND
SERVE WITH THE POTATO FRIES
AND VEGGIE STICKS.

SPRINKLE THE ADULTS' STEAKS WITH
THE SPICY SALT. COOK THE STEAKS
AND SERVE WITH THE GRILLED TOMATOES
AND ZUCCHINIS AND THE POTATO FRIES.

Crispy Yoghurt Chicken Legs

Panko crumbs add crunch and subtle spices jazz up this chicken dish making it a treat for adults. Crumb both the adults' and kids' versions and bake at the same time.

INGREDIENTS
250 g (9 oz/1 cup) Greek-style yoghurt
2 garlic cloves, crushed
juice of 1 lemon
6 chicken drumsticks (1 each for the kids, 2 each for the adults)
salt
120 g (4½ oz/2 cups panko crumbs)
6 teaspoons butter (1 for each leg)
salad, to serve

INGREDIENTS FOR ADULTS
1 teaspoon ground chilli
1 teaspoon ground cumin
1 teaspoon ground coriander

METHOD
Preheat the oven to 180°C (350°f/Gas4).

Combine the yoghurt, garlic and lemon juice in a bowl.

Sprinkle the chicken with salt.

1. **DISH ONE** Coat the kids' drumsticks with the yoghurt mixture then roll them in the panko crumbs. Put the chicken on a baking tray lined with baking paper and top each leg with a teaspoon of butter.

Cover the tray with foil and bake for 45 minutes. Remove the foil and cook for a further 15 minutes, or until the chicken is golden.

Serve with a crisp salad.

2. **DISH TWO** Add the spices to the remaining yoghurt mixture.

Coat the chicken with the spicy yoghurt and roll in the panko crumbs. Put the chicken on a baking tray lined with baking paper and top each leg with a teaspoon of butter. (If you're baking the spicy chicken on the same baking tray as the kids' drumsticks, insert a toothpick into the spicy ones so you can tell the difference.)

Cover the tray with foil and bake for 45 minutes. Remove the foil and cook for a further 15 minutes, or until the chicken is golden.

Serve with a crisp salad.

SERVES 4

Thai Pork & Fried Egg

I love Thai Takeaway but it's way too boombah!! This homemade version tastes like the real thing without the spooky hidden ingredients...and calories! The kids love the meat, rice and egg on its own.

INGREDIENTS
60 ml (2 fl oz/¼ cup) fish sauce
1 tablespoon soy sauce
1 tablespoon kecap manis
1 teaspoon brown sugar
80 ml (2½ fl oz/⅓ cup) olive oil
1 garlic clove, crushed
400 g (14 oz) minced (ground) pork
1 red onion, chopped
100 g (3½ oz) green beans, cut into 3 cm (1¼ inch) lengths
handful fresh basil, torn

4 eggs
steamed rice, to serve
4 baby bok choy (pak choy), steamed

INGREDIENTS FOR ADULTS
½ teaspoon sambal oelek (chilli paste)
2 tablespoons lime juice
1 tablespoon fish sauce
1 teaspoon sesame oil
½ teaspoon brown sugar
½ teaspoon sesame seeds, toasted

METHOD

Stir the fish sauce, soy sauce, kecap manis and sugar in a bowl until the sugar has dissolved.

Heat two-thirds of the oil in a wok over a high heat. Stir-fry the garlic and minced pork for 2–3 minutes, or until the pork begins to brown. Add the onion and beans and stir-fry for 2 minutes. Add the fish sauce mixture and cook for another 3–4 minutes, or until the liquid is reduced by half and the pork is cooked through. Remove the pork from the heat and stir through the basil.

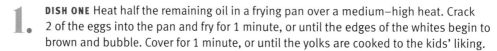

1. **DISH ONE** Heat half the remaining oil in a frying pan over a medium–high heat. Crack 2 of the eggs into the pan and fry for 1 minute, or until the edges of the whites begin to brown and bubble. Cover for 1 minute, or until the yolks are cooked to the kids' liking.

Top the pork with an egg and serve with the steamed rice and plain bok choy.

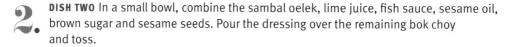

2. **DISH TWO** In a small bowl, combine the sambal oelek, lime juice, fish sauce, sesame oil, brown sugar and sesame seeds. Pour the dressing over the remaining bok choy and toss.

Heat the remaining oil in the frying pan and fry the remaining eggs until cooked to the adults' liking.

Top the pork with a fried egg and serve with the baby bok choy.

SERVES 4

1.
STIR-FRY MINCED PORK WITH FISH
SAUCE, SOY SAUCE AND KECAP MANIS.
SERVE ON A BED OF STEAMED RICE AND
TOP WITH A FRIED EGG.

2.
DRESS THE BOK CHOY WITH SAMBAL
OELEK, LIME, FISH SAUCE, SESAME OIL,
SUGAR AND SESAME SEEDS. SERVE
WITH THE PORK AND FRIED EGG.

Choco-Licious Pork Belly

This dish takes its cue from the great Mexican 'mole' sauces. The word chocolate evokes excitement for kids...the word chilli does it for me.

INGREDIENTS

1 carrot, quartered

2 onions, quartered

4 large garlic cloves

1 ×1 kg (2 lb 3 oz) boneless pork belly, skin left on and scored

2 teaspoons salt

Choco-licious sauce

1 cinnamon stick

3 tablespoons blanched almonds

2 tablespoons brown sugar

50 g (1¾ oz) dark chocolate (85% cocoa)

4 store-bought soft corn tortillas

INGREDIENTS FOR ADULTS

1 whole dried chipotle chilli

1 whole dried ancho chilli

Coriander and lime rice

370 g (13 oz/2 cups) steamed white rice

handful chopped coriander (cilantro) leaves

2 tablespoons lime juice

1 small red chilli, seeded and finely chopped

salt

METHOD

Preheat the oven to 180°C (350°F/Gas 4). Put the carrot, onions and garlic in a roasting tin. Rub the pork all over with salt, and place it on the vegetables. Pour enough water into the tin so the level rises to just under halfway up the pork belly. Cover the tin with foil and bake for around 1¼ hours.

Remove the foil and increase the heat to 220°C (430°F/Gas 7). Cook the pork for about 15 minutes, or until the skin crackles. Remove the pork to a tray and rest. Reserve 500 ml (17 fl oz/2 cups) of the roasting tin juices for the choco-licious sauce. Discard the solids.

In a frying pan over a medium heat, toast the cinnamon stick and almonds, stirring constantly, for about 5–6 minutes, or until the almonds are golden and the cinnamon is fragrant. Allow to cool, then finely chop in a small food processor or blender. Add the sugar and chocolate then pulse again. Divide the mixture and set half aside.

1. **DISH ONE** In a saucepan, bring 250 ml (8½ fl oz/1 cup) of the reserved roasting juices to the boil, then reduce the heat to low. Add one portion of the chocolate mixture and simmer, stirring occasionally, for about 3 minutes, or until the chocolate melts. Cook for a further 3 minutes, or until the sauce thickens. Serve slices of the pork in warmed corn tortillas and drizzle with the chocolate sauce.

2. **DISH TWO** In a saucepan, bring the remaining roasting tin juices and the chillies to the boil, then reduce the heat to low and simmer for 4 minutes. Add the remaining chocolate mixture and simmer, stirring occasionally, until the chocolate melts. Cook for a further 3 minutes, or until the sauce thickens. Strain the sauce and keep warm.

To make the coriander and lime rice, combine the rice, coriander, lime juice and chilli, and season with salt. Serve the rice with slices of pork, drizzled with the choco-licious sauce.

SERVES 6

1

ADD THE CHOCOLATE TO THE ROASTING
JUICES AND SIMMER. SERVE THE PORK IN
WARMED CORN TORTILLAS AND DRIZZLE
WITH THE CHOCOLATE SAUCE.

SIMMER THE CHILLIES, ROASTING
JUICES AND CHOCOLATE TO MAKE
THE CHOCO-LICIOUS SAUCE. DRIZZLE
THE SAUCE OVER THE PORK AND SERVE
WITH THE CORIANDER AND LIME RICE.

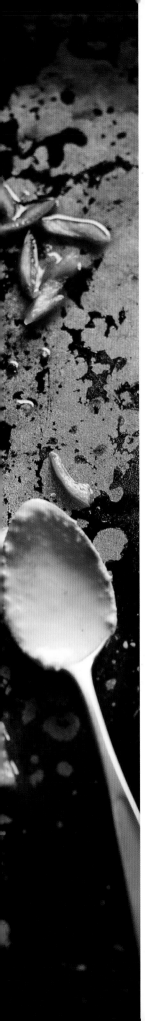

Pork Chops & Purple Slaw

My kids would eat lamb chops every single night if they could, but they're so expensive! I've steered them towards pork chops instead and they LOVE THEM. I serve this with a colourful purple coleslaw, spicing up the adult version with green chillies and wasabi mayonnaise.

INGREDIENTS
2–3 tablespoons olive oil
4 thick pork chops on the bone or cutlets
salt
lemon, to serve

Purple slaw
60 g (2 oz/¼ cup) mayonnaise
60 g (2 oz/¼ cup) Greek-style yoghurt
¼ purple cabbage, shredded
1 green apple, thinly sliced
juice of ½ lemon

INGREDIENTS FOR ADULTS
2 spring onions (scallions), finely shredded
handful flat-leaf (Italian) parsley, chopped
wasabi paste, to taste
1 large green chilli, finely chopped
1 quantity Horseradish hot 'creamy' sauce
   (page 23)

METHOD
Preheat the oven to 180°C (350°F/Gas 4).

Heat the olive oil in an ovenproof frying pan, or roasting pan, over a medium heat. Season the pork with salt and cook for about 5 minutes then turn and cook on the other side for a further 3–4 minutes.

Put the pan into the oven and bake for about 10 minutes, or until the chops or cutlets are cooked through.

1. **DISH ONE** For the kids' slaw, combine half the mayo and half of the yoghurt in a bowl. Add half the cabbage and half the apple, squeeze over a little lemon juice and toss to coat the cabbage well.

For the kids, serve the chops with the plain cabbage and apple salad.

2. **DISH TWO** To the remaining cabbage and apple, add the spring onion and parsley. Combine the remaining mayo and yoghurt with the lemon juice and wasabi. Stir through the slaw and top with the chilli.

Top the adults' chops with a dollop of horseradish cream and serve with the spicy cabbage slaw.

SERVES 4

Cool Veggies

As I've said before, I've never been crazy
about hiding vegetables in kids' food...I'd rather
they learn to like the taste. But sometimes
green bits and orange bits freak kids out.
Here are some really crunchy tasty
veggie recipes kids AND
grown-ups will love.

Zucchini & Carrot Fritters

My guys love these and are happy to eat them on their own as a meal. They also make another ripping hors d'oevres for parties. The creamy yoghurt sauce has plenty of kick as well to keep the adults double-dipping.

INGREDIENTS
185 g (6½ oz/1¼ cups) plain
   (all-purpose flour
2 teaspoons caster (superfine) sugar
1 teaspoon salt, plus extra to serve
½ teaspoon baking powder
½ teaspoon bicarbonate of soda
2 large eggs, separated
1 cup milk
30 g (1 oz) unsalted butter, melted
   and cooled
1 large zucchini, peeled and grated
2 carrots, grated
3 spring onions (scallions), chopped
3 garlic cloves, crushed
large handful flat-leaf (Italian) parsley,
   chopped
peanut oil, for frying

INGREDIENTS FOR ADULTS
¼ teaspoon ground cumin
¼ teaspoon ground coriander
¼ teaspoon chilli powder
125 g (4½ oz/½ cup) Greek-style yoghurt
squeeze of lemon juice
chopped red chilli, to serve
chopped coriander (cilantro) leaves, to serve

METHOD
Whisk together the flour, sugar, salt, baking powder, bicarbonate of soda, egg yolks and milk. Add the butter and whisk again. Combine the zucchini, carrot, spring onion, garlic and parsley and add it to the batter. Beat the egg whites until soft peaks form. Fold the egg whites into the zucchini and carrot mixture in two batches.

Preheat a non-stick frying pan over a medium–high heat and brush it with peanut oil. Using a ladle, scoop the batter into the pan. Cook for 2–3 minutes and flip.

Cook for a further 2 minutes and remove to a plate lined with paper towel. Continue until all the batter is cooked.

DISH ONE Sprinkle the fritters with salt and serve to the kids.

DISH TWO Mix together the cumin, ground coriander, chilli powder, yoghurt and lemon juice. Serve the fritters with a dollop of the spiced yoghurt and garnish with the fresh chilli and coriander.

MAKES 16 FRITTERS

1.

SPRINKLE THE FRITTERS WITH
SALT AND SERVE TO THE KIDS.

2.

COMBINE THE CUMIN, GROUND CORIANDER,
CHILLI POWDER, YOGHURT AND LEMON JUICE.
SERVE THE FRITTERS WITH THE SPICED
YOGHURT AND GARNISH WITH FRESH CHILLI
AND CORIANDER.

Beetroot & Carrot Salad with Cashews

This is a delicious side dish to any of the meat and fish recipes. Serve the kids the grated carrot, beetroot and sultanas and add the dressing and fresh herbs to the adult version.

INGREDIENTS
4 carrots, grated
2 beetroots, grated
60 g (2 oz/½ cup sultanas)

INGREDIENTS FOR ADULTS
1 clove garlic, peeled and left whole
60 ml (2 fl oz/¼ cup) white wine vinegar
80 g (2¾ oz/½ cup) unsalted cashews
60 ml (2 fl oz/¼ cup) lemon juice
80 ml (2¾ fl oz/⅓ cup) olive oil
½ cup loosely packed flat-leaf (Italian) parsley, chopped
3 tablespoons chopped mint leaves
½ teaspoon chilli flakes
salt and freshly ground black pepper

METHOD
Combine the carrots and beetroot in a bowl then remove half to another bowl.

1. **DISH ONE** Stir half of the sultanas through one bowl of the beetroot and carrot mixture and serve to the kids.

2. **DISH TWO** Combine the garlic, vinegar and remaining sultanas in a large bowl. Let the mixture sit for about 30 minutes then remove the garlic and discard.

Meanwhile, toast the cashews in a heavy-based frying pan over a medium heat, stirring frequently, until the nuts have just started to brown, about 2–3 minutes. Remove the cashews to a plate and let them cool.

To the remaining bowl of carrots and beetroot, add the vinegar mixture, lemon juice, olive oil, parsley, mint, chilli flakes, cashews and salt and pepper to taste. Combine well and serve.

SERVES 4

Warm Edamame Beans with Sea Salt

Frozen edamame beans can be found in the freezer section of Asian grocery stores.

Simply heat the beans in boiling salted water for about 4–5 minutes, drain, sprinkle with sea salt and serve with soy sauce for dipping.

Lemony Broccoli & Asparagus Tempura Spears

I love the idea of tempura veggies. It's so easy to make the batter. These are best served hot, so make the adults' and kids' dipping sauces before you start frying.

INGREDIENTS
vegetable oil, for deep-frying
150 g (5½ oz/1 cup) plain (all-purpose) flour
175 g (6 oz/1 cup) rice flour
500 ml (17 fl oz/2 cups) icy-cold water
zest of 1 lemon
200 g (7 oz) broccoli, cut into small florets
200 g (7 oz) asparagus, trimmed
Dipping sauce
60 ml (2 fl oz/¼ cup) soy sauce
60 ml (2 fl oz/¼ cup) lemon juice
3 teaspoons rice vinegar
2 teaspoons sesame oil

INGREDIENTS FOR ADULTS
1 tablespoon finely grated daikon
1 teaspoon finely grated ginger
¼ teaspoon red chilli flakes

METHOD
Mix together the dipping sauce ingredients and divide into two small bowls.

Heat the oil in a wok over a medium heat. The oil temperature should be around 190°C (375°F).

Meanwhile, make the tempura batter. In a large mixing bowl, whisk together the flours and water until combined. Stir through the lemon zest.

Add the broccoli to the batter and coat well. Use a slotted spoon to remove a few florets at a time and allow the excess batter to drip off. Place the spoon with the battered broccoli into the oil. Carefully remove the spoon and fry the broccoli, turning once, until the batter is golden brown and the broccoli is just tender, about 2–3 minutes. Drain the broccoli tempura on paper towel. Repeat with the remaining broccoli and the asparagus spears.

1. **DISH ONE** Serve the kids the broccoli and asparagus tempura with one of the bowls of the reserved dipping sauce.

2. **DISH TWO** To the adults' dipping sauce, add the daikon, ginger and chilli flakes and stir. Serve with the tempura broccoli and asparagus.

SERVES 4

Fresh Corn Tempura

Wicked. Crunchy. Crispy. Salty. Not for every day but an excellent treat for everyone. These are best served straight away, so make the minty dipping sauce for the adults before you start cooking. And a word of warning...don't stand directly over the wok as the hot oil will probably make the corn pop!

INGREDIENTS
1 corn cob, husk removed
vegetable oil for deep-frying
75 g (2¾ oz/½ cup) plain (all-purpose) flour, plus extra for dusting
90 g (3 oz/½ cup) rice flour
250 ml (8½ fl oz/1 cup) icy-cold water

INGREDIENTS FOR ADULTS
125 g (4½ oz/½ cup) Greek-style yoghurt
small handful mint, very finely chopped
squeeze of lemon juice
pinch of salt

METHOD
Cut the corn kernels from the cob.

Heat the oil in a wok over a medium heat. The oil temperature should be around 190°C (375°F).

While the oil is heating, prepare the batter. Whisk together the flours and water until the batter is combined, but still a touch lumpy.

Dust the corn kernels with a little flour and add them to the batter. Use a slotted spoon to remove a small amount of battered corn. Allow the excess batter to drip off, then place the spoon with the batter into the oil. Carefully remove the spoon and fry the corn cake for 2–3 minutes, turning once.

While the corn cake is frying, use the slotted spoon to remove another small amount of batter and repeat the process. Be careful not to overcrowd the wok.

When the cakes are crispy and golden, remove to a plate lined with paper towel.

 DISH ONE Serve the kids the crunchy corn cakes as they are.

 DISH TWO Combine the yoghurt, mint, lemon juice and salt in a bowl. Serve the minty yoghurt dip with the hot corn cakes.

MAKES ABOUT 15 CORN CAKES

Pancakes with Peas

A delicious way to serve peas...in pancakes drizzled with butter.
Although, I like to top mine with some Greek yoghurt instead of butter.

INGREDIENTS
3 large eggs
250 g (9 oz/1 cup) low-fat cottage cheese
35 g (1¼ oz/¼ cup) plain flour
2 tablespoons vegetable oil
½ teaspoon salt
155 g (5½ oz/1 cup) frozen peas, thawed and
  drained
90 g (3 oz) unsalted butter, melted

INGREDIENTS FOR ADULTS
2 spring onions (scallions), thinly sliced,
  plus extra to serve
½ teaspoon ground coriander
½ teaspoon ground cumin
Greek-style yoghurt, to serve

METHOD
Combine the eggs, cottage cheese, flour, vegetable oil and salt in a blender and
process until smooth. Transfer to a bowl and stir in the peas.

Divide the mixture into two bowls.

1. DISH ONE Heat a large non-stick frying pan over a low heat and add half a teaspoon
of the melted butter. Use a ladle to scoop the pancake mixture into the pan. Cook
the pancake for about 3 minutes, or until it starts to bubble on top. Turn and cook on
the other side for 2 minutes, or until browned and cooked through. Repeat with the
remaining batter.

Drizzle with a little melted butter and serve to the kids.

2. DISH TWO Mix the spring onions, coriander and cumin through the other bowl of batter.

Heat a large non-stick frying pan over a low heat and add half a teaspoon of the melted
butter. Use a ladle to scoop the pancake mixture into the pan. Cook the pancake for
about 3 minutes, or until it starts to bubble on top. Turn and cook on the other side for
2 minutes, or until just browned and cooked through. Repeat with the remaining batter.

Scatter over some spring onions and serve with a dollop of yoghurt.

MAKES ABOUT 10 PANCAKES

1.
COOK THE PEA PANCAKES THEN
DRIZZLE WITH MELTED BUTTER
AND SERVE TO THE KIDS.

2.
ADD SPRING ONION, CUMIN AND
CORIANDER TO THE ADULTS' PANCAKES.
GARNISH WITH SPRING ONION AND
SERVE WITH A DOLLOP OF YOGHURT.

Mamasita Corn on the Cob

This recipe comes from my favourite Mexican restaurant, Mamasita.
It's so popular the long staircase is lined with people every night. I use
parmesan instead of Mexican cheese, which works fine.

INGREDIENTS
6 corn cobs, husks removed, cut in half
125 g (4½ oz/½ cup) mayonnaise
juice of ½ lime
1 tablespoon olive oil
100 g (3½ oz/1 cup) grated parmesan
lime wedges, to serve

INGREDIENTS FOR ADULTS
1 teaspoon cayenne pepper
2 teaspoons sweet smoked paprika
2 teaspoons salt
2 chipotle chillies or 2 tablespoons chipotle
  sauce or 1–2 teaspoons chipotle chilli
  powder

METHOD

Bring a large saucepan of water to the boil. Cook the corn for 1 minute, then drain.

Combine the mayonnaise and lime juice then divide into two bowls.

Heat the grill of your barbecue or a chargrill pan to a very high heat. Brush the corn with olive oil then cook, turning regularly, for 10–12 minutes, or until charred and tender.

1. **DISH ONE** Insert a bamboo cocktail stick into one end of each of the kids' corn pieces. Brush the corn with the mayonnaise mixture, sprinkle with half the cheese and serve with lime wedges.

2. **DISH TWO** While the corn is grilling, combine the cayenne pepper, paprika and salt in a small bowl.

If using chipotle chillies, heat a small frying pan over a high heat then toast the chillies for about 30 seconds on each side, or until fragrant. Remove from the pan and discard the stems and seeds. Coarsely chop the chillies and grind them to a powder using a small food processor or a spice grinder.

Add the chipotle powder or sauce to the lime juice and mayonnaise mixture.

Insert a bamboo cocktail stick into one end of each of the adults' corn pieces. Brush the corn all over with the chipotle mayonnaise. Sprinkle with the paprika mixture and the remaining cheese and serve with lime wedges.

SERVES 6

1. COOK THE CORN UNTIL CHARRED AND TENDER. BRUSH WITH THE MAYONNAISE MIXTURE, SPRINKLE WITH PARMESAN AND SERVE WITH WEDGES OF LIME.

2. FOR ADULTS, CHARGRILL THE CORN THEN COAT WITH A CHIPOTLE MAYONNAISE. SPRINKLE WITH CAYENNE PEPPER, SMOKED PAPRIKA AND PARMESAN AND SERVE WITH LIME WEDGES.

Roasted Balsamic Beetroot with Orange & Feta

A gorgeous-looking grown-up salad. If your kids aren't into the whole green leaves and dressing caper, just give them wedges of juicy orange and salty feta – it works a treat in my house!

INGREDIENTS

4 beetroot (beets), unpeeled, tops trimmed off
1 tablespoon olive oil
salt and freshly ground black pepper
150 g (5½ oz) baby spinach
2 small pink or ruby grapefruits, peeled and cut into segments, white pith and membranes removed
2 oranges, peeled and cut into segments, white pith and membranes removed
150 g (5½ oz/¾ cup) crumbled feta
3 tablespoons snipped chives

Dressing

2½ tablespoons balsamic vinegar
2 teaspoons dijon mustard
2 teaspoons grated orange zest
2 teaspoons grated grapefruit zest
1 teaspoon honey
80 ml (2½ fl oz/⅓ cup) olive oil

METHOD

Preheat the oven to 200°C (400°F/Gas 6). Toss the beetroot and oil in a large bowl and season with salt and pepper. Wrap each beetroot in foil. Put them on a baking tray and roast for 1–1¼ hours, or until cooked through.

While the beetroots are roasting, whisk together all the dressing ingredients, except the oil, in a bowl. Slowly whisk in the oil. Season with salt and pepper.

When the beetroot are ready, remove them from the oven and open the foil. Let them cool for 30 minutes then gently rub off the skins. Cut them into wedges and season with salt and pepper.

Combine the spinach with 2 tablespoons of the dressing in a large bowl. Arrange the spinach on a platter.

Toss the beetroot and grapefruit and orange segments with 2 tablespoons of the dressing in the same bowl. Top the spinach with the beetroot wedges and citrus segments, and scatter over the feta and chives.

Acknowledgements

You folks at Hardie Grant really are a lovely bunch. Special thanks to Publishing Director Paul McNally for your incredible patience, faith and subtle prodding in encouraging me to write this third book. You were so enthusiastic from the get go. Thanks also to the positive force of nature that is Helen Withycombe, a fabulous, fun editor who said 'yes' to all my kooky dish suggestions. Meelee Soorkia, I so appreciated your precise, concise and spot on suggestions and questions, particularly with regard to my random serving sizes! Trish Garner thank you... you've absolutely nailed it again with your gorgeous design and helped me create exactly the vision I had for this family book. I'm rapt.

I'm so lucky to have been able to continue to work with the very talented Mark Roper. You're so much fun to work with and your photos are simply stunning. I was thrilled to again enjoy the extraordinary creative skills of Deborah Kaloper who styled such beautiful pictures. Thank you so much. Caroline Griffiths you were a delight to have run my kitchen and thank you for cooking up an absolute storm.

Thanks always to my second family at Working Dog, my mum and dad for their spectacular grandparenting skills and my first, funny, hungry family at home.

Index